Successful Summer Reading Programs for All Ages

PRACTICAL GUIDES FOR LIBRARIANS

About the Series

This innovative series written and edited for librarians by librarians provides authoritative, practical information and guidance on a wide spectrum of library processes and operations.

Books in the series are focused, describing practical and innovative solutions to a problem facing today's librarian and delivering step-by-step guidance for planning, creating, implementing, managing, and evaluating a wide range of services and programs.

The books are aimed at beginning and intermediate librarians needing basic instruction/guidance in a specific subject and at experienced librarians who need to gain knowledge in a new area or guidance in implementing a new program/service.

About the Series Editor

The **Practical Guides for Librarians** series was conceived by and is edited by M. Sandra Wood, MLS, MBA, AHIP, FMLA, Librarian Emerita, Penn State University Libraries.

M. Sandra Wood was a librarian at the George T. Harrell Library, the Milton S. Hershey Medical Center, College of Medicine, Pennsylvania State University, Hershey, PA, for over thirty-five years, specializing in reference, educational, and database services. Ms. Wood worked for several years as a development editor for Neal-Schuman Publishers.

Ms. Wood received an MLS from Indiana University and an MBA from the University of Maryland. She is a fellow of the Medical Library Association and served as a member of MLA's Board of Directors from 1991 to 1995. Ms. Wood is founding and current editor of *Medical Reference Services Quarterly*, now in its thirty-fifth volume. She also was founding editor of the *Journal of Consumer Health on the Internet* and the *Journal of Electronic Resources in Medical Libraries* and served as editor/coeditor of both journals through 2011.

Titles in the Series

Successful Summer Reading Programs for All Ages

A Practical Guide for Librarians

Katie Fitzgerald

PRACTICAL GUIDES FOR LIBRARIANS, NO. 39

ROWMAN & LITTLEFIELD
Lanham • Boulder • New York • London

Published by Rowman & Littlefield
An imprint of The Rowman & Littlefield Publishing Group, Inc.
4501 Forbes Boulevard, Suite 200, Lanham, Maryland 20706
www.rowman.com

Unit A, Whitacre Mews, 26-34 Stannary Street, London SE11 4AB

British Library Cataloguing in Publication Information Available

Library of Congress Cataloging-in-Publication Data Available

ISBN 978-1-4422-8167-7 (pbk. : alk. paper) | ISBN 978-1-4422-8168-4 (ebook)

♾™ The paper used in this publication meets the minimum requirements of American National Standard for Information Sciences—Permanence of Paper for Printed Library Materials, ANSI/NISO Z39.48-1992.

Printed in the United States of America

For Elizabeth,

who shared a due date with this book.

Contents

Figures and Tables

 Figures

Tables

Preface

For over a century, youth services librarians have spent their summers promoting reading to their young patrons and working to prevent a loss of reading skills during the summer months. In past decades, these summer reading programs may have been as simple as one children's librarian putting up a bulletin board for independent readers in elementary school or very young children being asked to draw pictures based on their favorite stories. Though these specific approaches may not be as popular anymore, given the ever-evolving nature of public libraries, summer reading programs in some form continue to be the focal point of most libraries' years. As times have changed, more staff members have also become involved in planning these programs. Whereas in the past summer reading programs were the domain of the children's librarian, today librarians from all departments frequently work together to provide summer reading programs for patrons of all ages.

In recent years, public libraries across the United States have become much more focused not just on the literacy skills of school-age children but on the value of reading as a lifelong pastime and the role of the library in the lives of its patrons. A survey of articles published in professional and news publications in recent years reveals a variety of interesting approaches libraries are using to encourage patrons to read and use the library from childhood through adulthood. On November 1, 2016, Tony Spinelli of Wilton Connecticut's *Wilton Bulletin* published "Kids Loving the Library," an article about the Wilton Library's decision to allow library cards to be issued to children from birth rather than insisting that these young patrons wait until they turn five years old. On April 18, 2017, *Public Libraries Online* reporter Andrew Hart interviewed Jenny Adams Perinovic, outreach coordinator at the Free Library of Philadelphia, about the Field Family Teen Author Series, which aims to foster personal connections between teens and the authors of the books they read. The June 1, 2017, issue of *Library Journal* highlighted the work of Tysha Shay, a reference manager at a branch of Missouri's Springfield-Greene County Library District, whose program Stories for Life brings books and other library materials to Alzheimer's patients. Each of these programs represents a trend in public library service toward connecting readers with books during all phases of life and not just during the school years.

As summer reading programs expand to accommodate this broader view of literacy, the burden on library staff also increases. With more patrons involved in summer reading than ever before, many libraries are consumed nearly year-round with the process of putting together an exciting summer program. Sometimes staff cannot even find the time to regroup between the end of one program and the beginning of the next. *Successful Summer Reading Programs for All Ages: A Practical Guide for Librarians* has been written with the goal of streamlining and simplifying the process of planning summer reading programs in order to ease some of the burden on library staff. This book gathers in a single volume all of the basic information needed to organize, plan, implement, evaluate, and troubleshoot a summer reading program for all age groups without needing to reinvent everything from scratch each year. It provides a sense of direction and focus from which you can then branch out to personalize your program to your own individual library.

⊚ Organization of This Book

Successful Summer Reading Programs for All Ages: A Practical Guide for Librarians includes nine chapters, each of which focuses on a different facet of the summer reading planning process. Every chapter provides suggestions and best practices that can be adapted for use in any public library setting.

Chapter 1, "Summer Reading Basics," defines summer reading programs and identifies the key reasons that libraries continue to offer them. It provides an overview about adding special events to a summer reading program and briefly touches on budgeting concerns.

Chapter 2, "Developing a Summer Reading Program," provides a road map for planning your library's specific summer reading program. It walks you through the process of setting goals, determining who will participate, identifying the most efficient way to register patrons, working with or without a theme, and selecting the format for your program. It also includes a useful timeline of tasks to complete in order to be properly prepared for the start of your program each year.

The middle chapters of the book—chapter 3, "Summer Reading Programs for Early Childhood (Ages 0–5)"; chapter 4, "Summer Reading Programs for School-Age Children (Ages 6–12)"; chapter 5, "Summer Reading Programs for Teens"; and chapter 6, "Summer Reading Programs for Adults"—discuss the needs of each specific audience for which you might offer a summer reading program and provide suggestions for activities and prizes that appeal to each.

Chapter 7, "Promoting Your Summer Reading Program," provides information about the many ways you can get the word out about summer reading, including printed material, website content, social media platforms, neighborhood email lists, and visits to local schools.

Chapter 8, "Evaluating Your Summer Reading Program," identifies ways to determine whether your summer reading program has been a success and suggests how your evaluation can be used to make decisions about future programs.

Finally, chapter 9, "Solving Summer Reading Problems," uses a question-and-answer format to address some of the common problems that might arise during a summer reading program, with real-world suggestions for defusing each difficult situation.

◎ How to Use This Book

The chapters of *Successful Summer Reading Programs for All Ages: A Practical Guide for Librarians* are organized in a logical progression, so if you are brand-new to summer reading programs, you can read the book straight through and experience an entire crash course in how best to put together your program. If you only want to focus on improving one or two aspects of your summer reading program, or if you are expanding your program to include a new age group, each chapter can also stand on its own as a complete lesson on its area of focus. The program ideas listed in each age-group-specific chapter may also be of interest to any librarian, regardless of experience, and supervisors will be especially interested in chapter 8, "Evaluating Your Summer Reading Program."

Overall, this book is intended as a summer reading companion that will help you make decisions efficiently, organize events easily, resolve problems quickly, and alleviate at least some of the stresses and difficulties associated with planning summer reading programs.

Acknowledgments

I would like to thank Sandy Wood and Charles Harmon for their helpful feedback throughout the writing process. Thanks also to Ginny Neidermier and the staff of the Josephine-Louise Public Library for making possible many of the experiences that informed the writing of this book.

Additionally, I would like to express my appreciation to my husband, Michael, for the advice and assistance he gave for each chapter and for patiently wrangling our children while I worked to meet my deadlines.

Summer Reading Basics

I F YOU WERE A LIBRARY USER AS A CHILD or have been the parent or grandparent of a child who regularly uses the library, you have probably heard something about summer reading programs. You may associate these programs with reading logs and stickers, treasure chests of plastic prizes, end-of-summer ice cream parties, and bulletin boards bearing the names of star readers. Though these elements are still present in many of today's summer reading programs, there is also much more to a twenty-first-century summer reading program than simply reading for rewards. This chapter will provide you with the basic foundational knowledge you will need to understand what a summer reading program involves and why reading during the summer is so important.

What Is a Summer Reading Program?

For those who have not worked in libraries before or who have never assisted with a summer reading program, it may seem obvious that such a program is simply about encouraging your patrons, especially children, to read. While this may have been true in years past, the definition of a summer reading program has evolved significantly over the decades. Today, the phrase "summer reading" suggests to librarians not just a reading contest that takes place during the summer months but a well-developed and carefully structured set of activities designed to promote the library's materials, services, and in-house resources along with the value of reading. When you undertake the task of developing a successful summer reading program, you are setting out to create an entire calendar of summer events and activities that will appeal to patrons of all ages and that will encourage reading and library use in your community.

In the twenty-first century, summer reading programs can include almost anything a library can offer. Along with traditional reading contests, in recent years libraries have offered outdoor concerts and StoryWalks™, story times for everyone from babies to beginning readers, online photo challenges, teen volunteer programs, makerspace demonstrations, and even opportunities to read aloud to therapy dogs. Though reading remains the central focus of these programs, there is a growing emphasis on libraries as community gathering places, educational centers, and sources of entertainment that heavily influences how libraries develop their summer reading programs. As long as they involve reading and library use in some way, summer reading programs can be as unique as the libraries that offer them.

Why Offer Summer Reading Programs?

The American Library Association (ALA) has reported that 95 percent of public libraries offer summer reading programs (ALA, 2014). Why do so many libraries present these programs each summer? The primary reasons are connected to tradition, academics, and customer service.

Tradition

Summer reading programs have been a mainstay of library programming, particularly in children's departments, since before the turn of the twentieth century (Bertin, 2004). Several generations of readers have grown up using the library during the summer for academic purposes as well as for pleasure, and for many families and communities, the summer reading program is an intrinsic part of their summer experience. Though libraries have regularly reinvented summer reading programs to suit other changes in public libraries over time, it is no surprise that, at their heart, these programs remain focused on enjoying both the act of reading and the library itself.

In many situations, continuing a library program year after year out of loyalty to a tradition is not a good idea. Insisting upon continuing certain practices simply because "we have always done them this way" often results in frustration for staff, dissatisfaction for patrons, and stagnation for the library as a whole. When you consider tradition as it applies to summer reading programs, you should not attempt to offer the exact same program year after year. Instead, you simply want to be aware of how summer reading has impacted your community. If the summer reading program has been a part of your patrons' summer experience for many decades, eager participants will seek you out each year, pleased to see a program they love and enjoy continuing into the twenty-first century. Your community's sense of tradition surrounding summer reading can also help to build a strong group of participants each summer and can make it easier for the library to find community organizations to serve as partners and sponsors for the program.

Academics

Tradition aside, the main reason that promoting reading during the summer remains a priority of public libraries is a phenomenon known as summer learning loss or "the summer slide." Summer learning loss refers to students' loss of academic skills, including reading skills, during vacation from school. According to the National Summer Learning Association (NSLA), children from low-income families can "lose two to three months in reading" during the summer (NSLA, 2016a). The NSLA also notes that "summer learning loss can leave low-income students two-and-a-half to three years behind their peers" (NSLA, 2016b).

In 2011, when speaking on behalf of the Campaign for Grade-Level Reading at a U.S. Department of Education event, Annie E. Casey Foundation executive vice president Ralph Smith said of summer learning loss, "This is not a school problem; this is a community problem, and we've got to organize ourselves to solve that" (Smith, 2012). Since libraries continue to serve young patrons during the summer when schools are closed, they are in an especially advantageous position to help kids combat summer slide and to help them remain on grade level in reading even when school is not in session. Indeed, studies such as the Summer Reading Program Impact Study, conducted by the Library of Virginia and Virginia Department of Education from 2013 to 2015, have shown that library summer reading programs do have measurable positive impacts on academic performance. The Summer Reading Program Impact Study showed that "children and teens who attended summer reading programs performed better academically and experienced greater gains in their academic performance than their nonparticipating peers. Participants out-performed nonparticipants on tests across all measures and grades, kindergarten through 8" (Library of Virginia, 2015). The study also concluded that "summer reading programs may . . . even facilitate learning gains when schools are not in session" (Library of Virginia, 2015). Knowing the impact they can have on the students in their community, it only makes sense that libraries continue to offer and regularly improve upon their summer reading programs.

For patrons who are not students (young children, parents, senior citizens, etc.), there are still many benefits to developing and maintaining a regular reading habit, and libraries tap into these as well. Studies frequently cited by the Every Child Ready to Read initiative have highlighted the importance of helping young children to develop early literacy skills that will prepare them for learning to read. Many libraries offer story times and other activities to support these skills all year round but especially during the summer months, when demand for early childhood activities is often higher. Research has also reinforced the positive impact of reading on adults. Among other benefits, reading has been shown to slow the decline of memory in adults as they age (Wilson et. al., 2013) and to increase empathy in adult readers who connect emotionally with works of fiction (Bal and Veltkamp, 2013). Since libraries are home to reading material for all ages and interests, they are one of the best avenues for readers of all ages to encounter books and garner the benefits associated with reading.

Customer Service

Finally, summer reading programs continue to be a necessary part of library service because of the needs of the community. Many public and private schools now assign students reading projects to complete during the summer, and families often rely upon libraries to supply the required books. By offering their own reading programs during the summer, libraries make it clear that they are available to help kids with the reading they are assigned to do over vacation. Library programs also provide additional motivation for students to complete their assignments, since the library may reward them for each book read or for reaching a particular reading goal.

@ Beyond Reading

As mentioned above, summer reading programs are no longer just about reading. When you plan a summer reading program, you must also be prepared to develop supplemental activities to draw attention to your summer reading program and to keep your community engaged. There are three main reasons why library events outside of the reading challenge itself are such an important part of summer reading:

1. Competition. Especially in larger communities and urban areas, there are a lot of activities vying for the attention of your library patrons during the summer. In order to compete successfully with those other options, your program should be appealing and exciting. By offering a variety of events for the age groups served by your summer reading program, you provide an enticing, free alternative to some of the flashier events being offered by other organizations, and you give patrons a reason to visit the library aside from simply borrowing materials. When you increase the number of people who visit your library, you also increase the likelihood of those individuals learning about and participating in summer reading.
2. Education. Reading is not the only academic skill that suffers during the summer. Now that many libraries have access to makerspaces; STEAM (science, technology, engineering, arts, and mathematics) learning stations; and other educational tools not directly related to literacy, they have an opportunity to expand their services to kids and teens who are trying to maintain their skills over the summer. Since most patrons will not have access to tools of this type outside of the library (except maybe in school), these resources are valuable and will attract audiences that might not otherwise make use of the library.
3. Promotion. Often the summer months are busier for libraries than the other months of the year. Increased foot traffic in the library due to patrons borrowing reading material for the summer reading program provides a great opportunity for you to show off all that your library has to offer. Library events are the perfect way to highlight new technologies (such as a projection system for showing films or a 3-D printer available to the public), small and little-used collections (local history or books by local authors), and other resources and activities available through the library (databases, classes offered by library staff, clubs, group meetings, etc.).

Specific ways that libraries can go beyond reading in their summer reading programs will be discussed in detail in chapter 3, "Summer Reading Programs for Early Childhood (Ages 0–5)"; chapter 4, "Summer Reading Programs for School-Age Children (Ages 6–12)"; chapter 5, "Summer Reading Programs for Teens"; and chapter 6, "Summer Reading Programs for Adults."

@ Budgeting for a Summer Reading Program

Before you begin to plan a summer reading program, it is important to have a clear picture of your library's finances. Consider especially how much money is available for expenses like hiring performers, purchasing prizes, covering printing costs for promotional materials, paying for themed decorations, and acquiring any other supplies you may need that the library does not typically keep in stock.

In addition to any funds that your library might allocate specifically to the summer reading program, you might also consider requesting, soliciting, or applying for additional money from the Friends of the Library, grant programs, and/or local sponsors.

Friends of the Library

If your library has a Friends group, its members probably raise funds on behalf of the library all year round. If there is a particular expense you will not be able to cover using the library's summer reading budget alone, consider asking your Friends group to provide the necessary funding.

When you approach the Friends, first make sure to coordinate with your administration to ensure that your request for funds will not be competing with that of another librarian, department, or branch. This is especially important in larger libraries with many staff members and locations. Once your plan to apply for funding from the Friends has been approved, you should be prepared to make a short presentation describing the specific expense you would like them to cover, how funding this expense will benefit the patrons of your library, and how you will ensure that summer reading participants make use of the event, item, or activity you wish to provide. Expect to answer questions about your plans and to wait for the group to discuss the proposal in your absence before a final answer is given. When funding from your Friends group has been secured, be sure to thank them, not just with a card or note but also with public acknowledgment of their role in making possible the performance, event, or activity for which they provided funding. This helps to promote the Friends of the Library and also shows the library's gratitude for the work of the Friends' volunteers.

Sponsors

In addition to your Friends of the Library group, there may be other local businesses and organizations that would happily support your summer reading program. As you decide whom to approach, consider businesses and organizations in the following categories:

- Arts organizations
- Banks
- Bookstores
- Dance studios
- Fitness centers
- Insurance agencies
- Law practices
- Local radio and TV stations
- Local sports teams
- Medical groups
- Movie theaters
- Museums
- Music schools and shops
- Public and private schools
- Real estate agencies
- Restaurants
- Theater groups
- Toy stores
- Tutoring centers

Summer Reading Grants

There are a variety of federal, state, corporate, and nonprofit agencies that have grant money available for use by libraries that host summer reading programs. Below are a few examples of grants related to either summer reading or literacy in public libraries in general.

- Baker & Taylor Summer Reading Program Grant. The winning proposal for this grant is awarded $3,000 to use toward a theme-based public library summer reading program in a public library that involves children with physical or mental disabilities in innovative ways. Applicants must be personal members of both the ALA and the Association for Library Service to Children (ALSC). More information is available at www.ala.org/alsc/awardsgrants/profawards/bakertaylor.

- Dollar General literacy grants. Dollar General has several grant programs, including an Adult Literacy Grant for nonprofit organizations that provide help in adult basic education, GED or high school equivalency preparation, or English-language acquisition, as well as a Summer Reading Grant for libraries to help students in pre-K through twelfth grade who are "new readers, below grade level readers or readers with learning disabilities" (Dollar General Literacy Foundation, n.d.). More information about these grants can be found at www2.dollargeneral.com/dgliteracy/Pages/grant_programs.aspx.

- Ezra Jack Keats Mini-Grants. The Ezra Jack Keats Foundation offers funding of up to $500 to assist libraries in designing and implementing creative programs. There is a limit of one application per library, and projects should foster creative expression and interaction with a diverse community. The Ezra Jack Keats Foundation's mini-grant webpage is at www.ezra-jack-keats.org/section/ezra-jack-keats-mini-grant-program-for-public-libraries-public-schools.

- Library Services and Technology Act (LSTA) Grants to States program. Each year, the Grants to States program distributes more than $150 million to state library administrative agencies in each of the fifty states, the District of Columbia, the U.S. territories, and the Freely Associated States.

⊚ Key Points

As you begin to plan a summer reading program, it is important to have some basic background information:

- Today's summer reading programs are not just reading contests but well-developed and carefully structured sets of activities designed to promote the library's materials, services, and in-house resources along with the value of reading.
- The decision to continue offering summer reading programs arises from patrons' sense of tradition, libraries' interest in combating summer learning loss and promoting lifelong learning, and the need for customer service for students with assigned summer reading projects.
- Supplemental activities in addition to a reading contest are a key part of summer reading programs because they help libraries compete with other organizations' summer activities, they provide educational opportunities that the community may not otherwise have, and they help promote library resources and materials.
- When budgeting for a summer reading program, be sure you are aware of the finances available to you and of sources for supplementing your library's budget with funding from the Friends of the Library, community organizations, and grants.

This chapter has introduced you to the concept of a summer reading program and some of its key components. In chapter 2, you will learn more about the details of a successful summer reading program.

ⓖ References

ALA (American Library Association). 2014. "Digital Inclusion Survey: Executive Summary." ALA website. www.ala.org/research/sites/ala.org.research/files/content/initiatives/DI2014execsummary.pdf.

Bal, P. Matthijs, and Martijn Veltkamp. 2013. "How Does Fiction Reading Influence Empathy? An Experimental Investigation on the Role of Emotional Transportation." *PLOS ONE* 8, no. 1. http://journals.plos.org/plosone/article?id=10.1371/journal.pone.0055341.

Bertin, Stephanie. 2004. "A History of Youth Summer Reading Programs in Public Libraries." UNC School of Information and Library Science. https://ils.unc.edu/MSpapers/2977.pdf.

Dollar General Literacy Foundation. N.d. "Literacy Grant Programs." Dollar General Literacy Foundation website. www2.dollargeneral.com/dgliteracy/Pages/grant_programs.aspx.

Library of Virginia. 2015. "Summer Reading Program Impact Study." Library of Virginia website. www.lva.virginia.gov/lib-edu/ldnd/srp-impact/.

NSLA (National Summer Learning Association). 2016a. "At a Glance." www.summerlearning.org/at-a-glance/.

———. 2016b. "Why Summers Matter." www.summerlearning.org/the-challenge/.

Smith, Lorna. 2012. "Slowing the Summer Slide." *Resourceful School* 69, no. 4 (December 2011/January 2012). www.ascd.org/publications/educational-leadership/dec11/vol69/num04/Slowing-the-Summer-Slide.aspx.

Wilson, Robert S., Patricia A. Boyle, Lei Yu, et. al. 2013. "Life-Span Cognitive Activity, Neuropathologic Burden, and Cognitive Aging." *Neurology* 81, no. 4. www.neurology.org/content/81/4/314.

Developing a Summer Reading Program

MOST LIBRARIES OFFER SUMMER READING PROGRAMS in some form every year, so it is rare that you will ever need to develop a program from scratch, even as a new hire. Still, there may be times when you want to overhaul an existing program or begin serving a new demographic, and you will need to know where to begin. This chapter will give you an overview of the different aspects of a successful summer reading program.

Identifying Your Goals

When you set out to provide any type of program for your community, it is important to identify the goals you are striving to reach. Chapter 1, "Summer Reading Basics," has already established the overarching goals for any summer reading program: to promote a love of reading and to prevent students from falling victim to summer learning loss. Beyond this larger aspiration, however, there should also be some smaller, measurable goals to help guide your vision for a given year's program. As you determine your specific goals, consider the following areas:

- Circulation. Perhaps your library has trouble circulating items in a specific collection. Your summer program could include a focus on those materials so that circulation might increase. Maybe your library had an increase in circulation last summer and you would like to improve upon that number even more. By placing a greater emphasis on registering patrons for library cards and proactively promoting books in your collection, you might strive to improve your overall circulation. Since summer is often a public library's busiest season, it is a great time to place more of your materials in the hands of patrons who will enjoy them.
- Participation. Small summer reading programs with low attendance can be very effective for the patrons who participate, but most libraries are interested in reaching as many members of the community as possible. Participation goals give you the motivation to reach out to new groups within your community who might not be aware that you offer a summer reading program. They also help you avoid becoming complacent. If you have a core group of people who are very interested in summer reading each year, you can begin to feel as though your work is done without realizing there are potential participants waiting in the wings.
- Attendance at events. Though reading is the main focus of summer reading programs, attendance at library events is also a key component for many libraries. One of the goals you set for yourself might focus on an increase in attendance at specific types of programs or an overall increase in attendance across the board. Since summer reading tends to put you in direct contact with many patrons with whom you might otherwise never interact, it is a prime opportunity for you to promote the library's year-round events calendar, as well as any special summer activities you have planned.
- Partnerships. Summer reading provides great opportunities for networking and partnering with local organizations and individuals to bring new and interesting activities into the library. As you write up your list of summer goals, consider adding a focus on increasing the number of partnerships you have in the community and finding ways to involve community members in your summer events.

Above all, goals for summer reading should always reflect your library's mission statement and your community's values and needs.

Summer Reading Themes

A long-standing tradition in public library summer reading programs is the summer reading theme. Formerly, themes were determined by individual state libraries, but now they are primarily chosen for member states by consortia like the Collaborative Summer Library Program (CSLP), based in Mason City, Iowa, and iRead, based in Chicago, Illinois. Some individual libraries or library systems also opt to choose their own themes or to avoid themes altogether. Though it is perfectly possible to have a successful summer reading program without one, there are some benefits to using a theme:

- Opportunities to exchange ideas. When all the libraries in a system or consortium use the same theme, it becomes much easier to find ideas for books, activities, and events to go along with it simply because everyone is brainstorming around the same topic. Librarians tend to be collaborative by nature, so knowing that others might be looking for inspiration on a particular theme also prompts many libraries to post their ideas online or share them to email lists where they might not otherwise appear.
- Availability of resources. Both CSLP and iRead provide summer reading manuals for their member libraries that include reproducible clip art, certificates, reading logs, and other printed material to accompany the year's theme. Also available for purchase from these organizations are T-shirts and other merchandise branded with the logo for the summer theme. While libraries could certainly create their own materials with their own chosen theme, it is often easier, and less expensive, to order premade items. This is especially true in smaller libraries without marketing departments or large budgets.
- Inspiration for selecting events and activities. Each year, many wonderful ideas for library events circulate through the library community. If you have trouble narrowing down what you would like to offer during the summer, it can be helpful to use a theme as a guideline in making your selections. Themes can also sometimes serve to breathe new life into existing library activities by inspiring you to look at them from a fresh angle.
- Branding for promotional purposes. A theme, whether self-selected or chosen by a consortium, makes it easier to create advertising for your summer program. Thematic elements can inform everything from the design of your flyers to the look of your website's summer reading page to the prizes you offer for completing the program. Since you will have to think about branding even if you do not use a theme, it may be easier to stick with a theme than it is to create your own materials from scratch. Details on advertising your summer reading program will appear in chapter 7, "Promoting Your Summer Reading Program."

If you have chosen to work with a theme for your summer reading program, there are many ways to have fun with the year's given topic. A theme can inform every aspect of your summer reading program. Decorating the library's bulletin boards with displays related to the theme helps to promote the program and gives the library an atmosphere of excitement about reading. Dressing up as a character or mascot related to the theme grabs the attention of community members, especially children, and provides opportunities to go out and network with community organizations. Giving each age group an engaging team name with a thematic flair is another fun way to draw in potential participants. For example, for a beach theme, you might call your early childhood participants "swimmies" and their school-age counterparts "surfers" or "beach bums."

On the other hand, trying too hard to make everything fit the theme can cause you to become frustrated and burn out before the summer even begins. To give yourself a little more freedom, remember that part of every summer reading theme is reading, so any activity you offer that focuses on reading is automatically connected with the theme. This includes events like story time, book discussions, and author talks, even if the subject matter of these events is not directly related to the theme of your overall program. It also includes prizes, such as books, chances to win an e-reader, or bookstore gift cards.

Themes are useful tools, and you only need to use them insofar as they help you develop your program. Any time the theme becomes a nuisance, it is time to reconsider how you are implementing it.

Participants

Once you know the focus and theme for your summer reading program, you need to think about who you would like to participate. To identify potential participants, consider the patrons who use your library regularly. Are they mostly retired adults or families with small children? Do college students frequent your library when they are home for the summer, or is your library more likely a favorite haunt of new moms with infants? Also consider organizations that might use your library only during the summer, such as camps, daycares, specialized classes, and tutoring groups. By identifying the patrons who are likely to be interested in a summer reading program, you will give yourself a pretty good idea of which age groups you should definitely include and which you might have to work harder to reach. Then you can determine whether to offer programs only for specific age groups or a comprehensive program for all age groups, including early childhood, school-age readers, teens, and adults.

Serving Multiple Age Groups

Traditionally, summer reading has been directed mainly at students in the elementary grades, but twenty-first-century libraries increasingly offer programs that involve patrons of all ages, from birth through adulthood. The decision to offer programs for multiple age groups might come about in a number of ways. In small libraries, it is often a group decision made by the members of a small staff. In larger libraries, the decision may come from a director or administrator, with specific instructions on how the program is to be carried out. Regardless of who makes the decision, it is important for library staff to work together on creating one program that serves everyone and not several programs without any connection between them.

In order to distribute the work equitably and avoid confusion, it is a good idea to have staff or committee meetings regarding summer reading, during which specific age groups are assigned to specific staff members and tasks are divided evenly among those staff members. There should be an easy system in place for committee members to communicate with each other in between meetings and an overall focus on streamlining the program so that it runs smoothly for all departments and all patrons. At all times, members of this committee must be on the same page and have the same understanding of the program's goals and rules. When different departments are not in sync, the program quickly becomes stressful, for both staff and patrons.

As you make plans for each age group, also consider the needs of different patrons at different stages of life. More information on how to tailor a summer reading program for the needs of a specific age group will be covered in chapter 3, "Summer Reading Programs for Early Childhood (Ages 0–5)"; chapter 4, "Summer Reading Programs for School-Age Children (Ages 6–12)"; chapter 5, "Summer Reading Programs for Teens"; and chapter 6, "Summer Reading Programs for Adults."

Determining Age Ranges

No matter whom you decide to invite to participate in your summer reading program, you will need to clearly delineate how the age groups are to be divided. This should not be done arbitrarily but according to some predetermined system that is applied to every patron in the same way. A typical breakdown of age groups might look like this:

- Early childhood (ages 0 to 5)
- Elementary readers (ages 6 to 12)
- Teens (ages 13 to 17)
- Adults (ages 18 and up)

While you do want to avoid making exceptions for too many participants, because it can becoming confusing, there are situations where it is prudent to be flexible. An eighteen-year-old who has not yet graduated high school, for example, might be more comfortable participating in a teen summer reading program than in one for adults. By the same token, the twelve-year-old who reads only young adult books or who will turn thirteen halfway through the summer could be treated as a teen without unfairly impacting other participants. Adults with learning or developmental disabilities may also be more comfortable participating in a program for children or teens, and there is no reason to disallow them. The age breakdowns really only become useful when it comes to recommending books to readers, selecting age-appropriate prizes, and keeping statistics.

⊚ Registration

After identifying your participants, it is time to decide how they will register for your summer reading program. Libraries use a wide range of methods for this task, many of which are overly complex and involve far too much paperwork to be manageable during a busy time of year. This section will focus on simplifying this process as much as possible and making it easy to maintain participation statistics without placing an undue burden on library staff.

Registration Methods

Before you choose a registration method, you will need to assess whether your library is ready for a digital registration process or if it would be better to use a traditional pen-and-paper approach. Your decision will be influenced by a number of factors:

- Availability of technology. If your patrons are likely to have access to smartphones, Internet connections, and computers at home, an online option is more feasible than if your patrons can only access these items in the library. Even if the majority of your users do have Internet access at home, it is still important to think of the ones who do not and to consider how you might help a participant without the needed technology sign up for your program. If you do not have the staff or the available computers for patrons to use to register in the library, your library may not yet be ready to switch to online registration.
- Budget. Libraries with smaller budgets may find the copying fees for distributing paper forms more affordable than a software package. Larger systems, on the other

hand, might see a software package as a beneficial investment to improve the registration process. If your library cannot afford the expense of a new software package or needs the funding to meet another need at this time, you might serve your patrons better by sticking to a paper-and-pen sign-up method.

- Patron preferences. Some communities are more averse to technology than others. If your patrons have previously shown a distaste for registering for library programs online, it might not yet be time for your library to switch to an all-online process.
- Staffing. Paper registration forms need to be collected by a staff person in real time, while online registration forms can be collected electronically and accessed by a staff person after the registration process for a given patron is complete. Libraries that are short-staffed may find it less stressful for their staff members and their patrons to use an online registration method.
- Demographics. Different age groups have different relationships to technology. Teens might only sign up for the program if they can do so online, while some senior citizens might be nervous about signing up unless they can do so on paper. In certain situations, in order to maximize everyone's ability to participate, you might choose to offer different formats for different age groups.

If you do ultimately decide to use an online registration method for at least some of your patrons, there are a variety of options available. Table 2.1 shows some of the most popular software programs available for registering patrons. Not included are programs that can be used to register and track patrons' progress. These will be discussed later in this chapter.

Collecting Registration Information

Whichever method you choose, there are some best practices you should keep in mind when collecting registration information from patrons. First, you should collect only the information you need. Some libraries have standard forms that have been used for years and years that collect details the library never uses. It is fine to ask for a patron's name, age, address, reading interests, and so on, but only if there is a need for the library to have that information during this particular summer. Minimizing the information you request from patrons cuts down on the time it takes to sign up, and it also cuts down on the paperwork you have to handle, process, file, and later destroy and throw away. It also helps to protect your patrons' privacy if you do not ask them for information just for the sake of asking.

Depending on how your program is structured, and on the statistical data you will need to collect, registration may not even be necessary at all. For information such as the number of tracking sheets you distribute to patrons or the number of kids who participate from a particular age group, you could simply keep a tally sheet at your desk and make a mark in the appropriate column each time someone new joins the program. You can always collect personal information from those who complete the program at the time they finish, thereby only collecting the details you need when the need becomes readily apparent.

Bulk Registrations

One of the big challenges libraries face during summer reading is handling the registration of large groups of participants, such as summer camps, daycares, tutoring groups, and special classes. Rather than trying to register individual children from a group in the

Table 2.1. Event Registration Software for Library Programs

METHOD	DESCRIPTION	FEATURES
Google Forms	Google's free program for creating and analyzing surveys.	• Ability to collaborate with multiple staff members on a single form. • Automatic collection of survey responses in a Google spreadsheet, which can be sorted and/or edited.
Engaged Patrons Library Events	Provided by Engaged Patrons, a company dedicated to connecting libraries to their patrons online. Allows libraries to post their events to their library website and manage online registration for these events.	• All services are hosted by Engaged Patrons. • Services are free to libraries with annual incomes below $1 million. • Online registration is included at no additional cost. • Automatic email confirmations for patrons upon registration. • Integrates into the library's existing website. • No coding required.
Evanced Sign Up	Event calendar management tool powered by Evanced, a Demco company.	• Integrates seamlessly with library's website and ILS. • Customizable to suit library's desired configuration. • Provides patron reminders via email or text. • Offers new mobile-enabled interface.
Eventbrite	Web-based program for creating, managing, and promoting events of all types.	• Free to use for all events where no fee is collected. • Custom survey tool allows for collection of additional information from patrons. • Ability to edit events after their initial publication online.
EK Mars (formerly Event Keeper)	Web calendar subscription service provided to libraries, schools, cities, towns, houses of worship, etc., by Plymouth Rocket.	• Fee-based service. Standard service does not include event registration. • Provides email confirmation for each registrant. • Collects and saves registration data, which can be exported to an Excel spreadsheet. • Automatically displays events on Facebook and Twitter. • Allows 900 events, 30 notes, and 10 editors at any one time during the subscription year. • Allows events to be deleted upon completion to save space.
SurveyMonkey	Web-based service for creating and sending surveys.	• Basic service allows 10 questions, 100 responses, and 3 collectors per survey. Fee-based services provide increasingly more sophisticated features. • Collects contact information. • Tracks email responses. • Provides real-time results.
Trumba	Website calendar tool with built-in event registration.	• Minimum fee of $99.95 for primary services. • Sets registration deadlines. • Sends email to staff each time a new patron registers. • Customizable registration confirmation message.

typical way, it saves a lot of time if you allow bulk registration for these larger groups. This might be a single form to be filled out with the names of every participant in the group or a function of your chosen software package. Allowing bulk registration makes it more likely that larger groups will want to join the summer reading program, and it allows you to focus more on helping the individuals progress through the program and less on the logistics of getting them started.

Concluding the Registration Process

At the conclusion of the registration process, it is important to make it clear to patrons what they should do next. This is especially important for online registration forms, as a staff person may not be present during the registration process to assist the patron. If the patron must come in to a physical library location to pick something up in order to start participating, include a message with this information on the form. If the patron is supposed to pick up a prize at a certain point after registering, make that clear as well. While having a high number of registrants is desirable, it is even more desirable to have patrons who participate throughout the program. Patrons are more likely to do this if there is a clear logical progression from the registration process into the actual program itself.

ⓖ Reading and Rewards

After registration, it is time for your patrons to start reading. As they begin the program, your participants will need to know how much they are being asked to read and when and how they should report their reading progress to you. This section will address the decisions you will need to make as you develop this most significant piece of your summer reading program.

Challenges and Goals

All summer reading programs have the goal of encouraging participants to read, but how libraries challenge their patrons to do so can vary rather widely by location. Depending on a given library's goals and on the interests of its community, a summer reading program might challenge participants to read a certain number of books, pages, or minutes. The goals might be cumulative for the entire summer, or there might be benchmarks to mark patrons' progress on the way to fulfilling a larger goal. Some libraries might also incorporate other types of learning into their reading programs so that patrons also receive credits toward their goals if they attend library programs, participate in literacy activities, or enrich their reading with art projects, reviews, and other extension activities. There are six main formats you can use to organize your goals for your patrons and help them keep track of their progress: reading log, bingo card, game board, checklist, calendar, and digital software. This section describes each format and lists associated pros and cons.

Reading Log

A reading log is the most basic of summer reading reporting tools. It simply asks patrons to keep personal lists of the books they read during the program and then turn those lists in at the library to receive their rewards. Reading logs work best for programs where reading is the sole focus and there is no other means of progressing toward the end goal.

Using the reading log method, you can challenge your patrons to read a total number of books for the entire summer and give them a prize when they reach that goal. Another option is to leave the end goal open-ended and simply offer increasingly greater rewards for patrons who read increasingly higher numbers of titles. A reading log can also be useful when participants are challenged to read one title from each of several different genres, formats, or other librarian-selected categories, as long as you include a place on the log for patrons to indicate which category each title is meant to represent.

The advantages of the reading log approach are its simplicity and straightforwardness. There are no complicated instructions to follow and no detailed recordkeeping to frustrate busy patrons. Participants only need to know the titles and authors of the books they have read, without also having to remember to make a note of how many pages are in each one or how long it took them to finish a given book. The reading log can also serve as a souvenir of summer reading when the program comes to an end, which might appeal especially to families with young children.

There are some drawbacks to this approach, however. Basing summer reading progress on how many books a patron reads penalizes those participants who read more slowly or who choose to read very long books. This problem is especially pronounced in programs for children, since kids develop reading skills at different rates. In an effort to keep up with the number of books their peers are reading, kids may start to read shorter books just to increase their numbers rather than books they truly enjoy reading. Even voracious readers may find the recordkeeping overwhelming. Families who read even just a few picture books to their young children each day can find themselves with a lot of writing to do to keep their logs up to date. For these reasons, a reading log is probably best for use with adult patrons or as an optional addition to your program for those who want it.

Figure 2.1 shows an example of a basic reading log, which has been filled out to show the books read by a prereading child.

Bingo Card

The bingo card is a versatile reporting tool for summer reading programs because you can customize it for almost any goal and tracking method. To use this approach, create a five-by-five grid and print a summer reading task in each square. If your library uses a theme for summer reading, connect some of these activities to the theme in order to engage patrons and help with program branding. Challenge each patron to complete a certain number of activities in order to earn a reward. Tasks might include reading for a certain amount of time or in a certain place. They might ask patrons to read titles from a specific category or from a certain time period. In the case of young children, tasks could be directly related to early literacy skills. You could also assign an equal value to each square (one title read, one day of reading, etc.).

The appeal of this approach is how easy it is to use (for both patrons and librarians) and how little recordkeeping is required. After you design your bingo card, it can easily be tweaked and reprinted each summer to suit new themes and new tasks without having to make a lot of major changes. The rules of the program also never have to change since bingo can always be played the same way no matter which theme you might be using or which age group you might be serving. Participants will also experience less confusion about summer reading and ask fewer time-consuming questions since bingo is a familiar game to most people and is easily learned if not previously known.

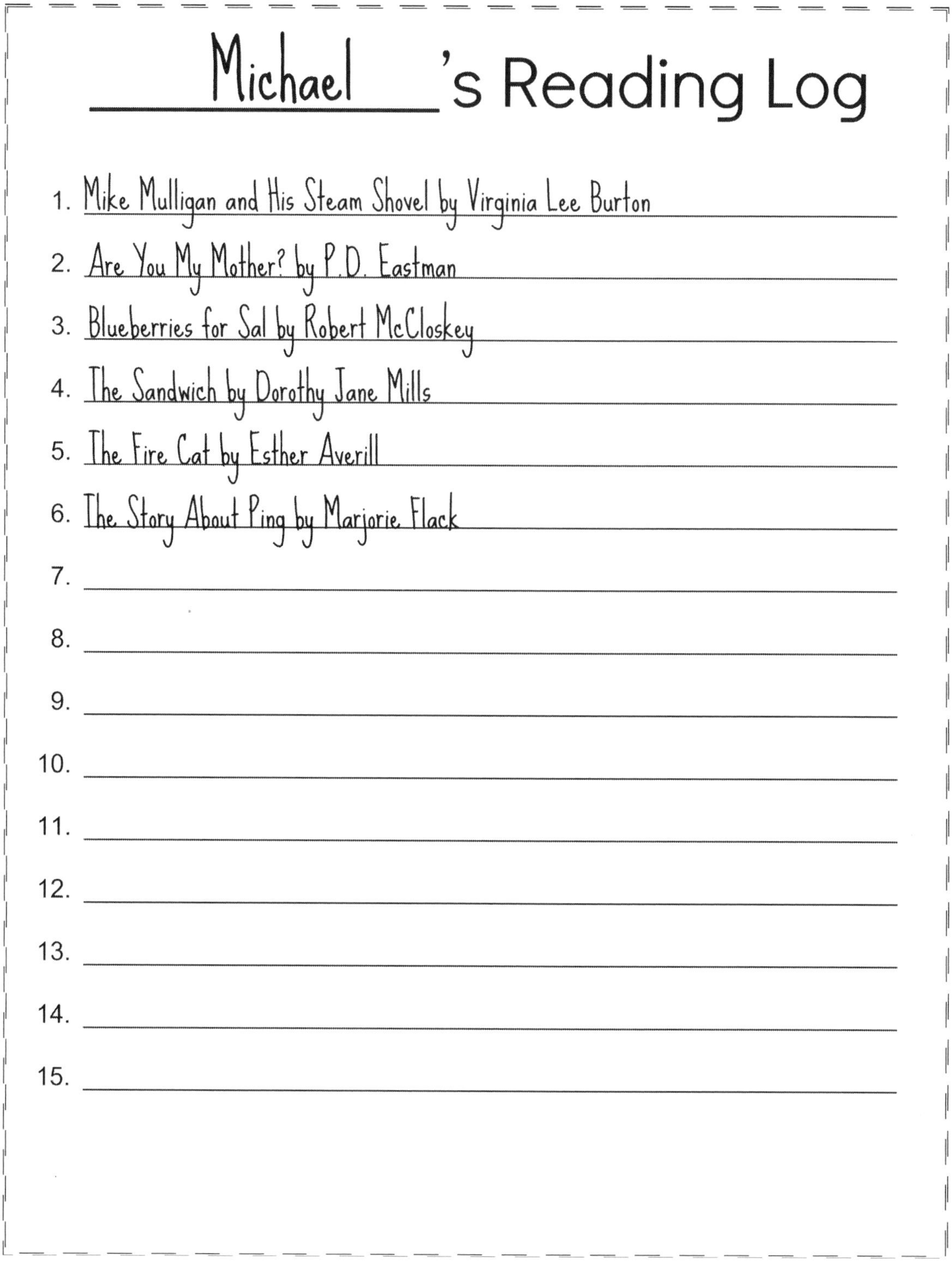

_____Michael_____'s Reading Log

1. Mike Mulligan and His Steam Shovel by Virginia Lee Burton

2. Are You My Mother? by P.D. Eastman

3. Blueberries for Sal by Robert McCloskey

4. The Sandwich by Dorothy Jane Mills

5. The Fire Cat by Esther Averill

6. The Story About Ping by Marjorie Flack

7. _____

8. _____

9. _____

10. _____

11. _____

12. _____

13. _____

14. _____

15. _____

Figure 2.1. Summer Reading Log. *Created by the author*

The main disadvantages of this approach involve patrons' views of your program. Potential summer reading program participants whose main interest is in reading, and not in reading-related tasks, might opt out of a program that asks them to do something more than read books. Participants might also feel that five tasks are too few and either avoid participating or finish quickly just to get the prize. Others might question the need to stop at five activities and hope for additional prizes for completing the full card. If you do choose to use a bingo card, it is usually wise to make it possible to win somehow by just reading books. You should also make patrons aware from the start of the summer whether there are any additional rewards associated with going above and beyond the set goal. Figure 2.2 shows a sample bingo card designed for an adult summer reading program.

READING BINGO

To complete the bingo challenge, read books that match the given categories, and mark off five boxes in a row in any direction. For an extra challenge, attempt to complete the entire card!

Graphic Novel	Biography	Book by an author you have never read before	Debut Novel	Award-winning Book
Poetry Collection	Romance Novel	Western Novel	Audiobook	Short Story Collection
Science Fiction Novel	Play	Sign Up for the Summer Reading Program	Celebrity Memoir	Bestseller
Mystery Novel	Book by an author who uses a pseudonym	Book published before 1950	Travel Book	True Crime Book
Book that has been translated	Classic	Fantasy Novel	Horror Novel	Book that has been made into a film

Figure 2.2. Summer Reading Bingo Card for Adults. *Created by the author*

Game Board

Game boards are similar to bingo cards, but they allow you the freedom to establish your own rules and format based on the specific needs and desires of your participants. Whatever specific layout you use for the physical game board itself, you will want to have a certain number of spaces and a clear means of progressing from space to space and ultimately toward the completion of the program. Depending on how you would prefer to track progress, you could set it up so that each space on the board is equivalent to a particular segment of time spent reading (fifteen minutes, for example), a particular number of books, or a day on the calendar. You could also assign point values to each space and provide a separate list of tasks, each of which is worth a specific number of points. If your program rewards patrons for reaching particular benchmarks, you can include these as spaces on the board, letting participants know in a printed message that when they surpass this particular space, they should stop by the library to claim a reward.

While the game board approach is one of the most fun to put together, it probably also requires the most work on the part of librarians. To create an appealing game board, you will need staff with both the graphic design skills to bring your vision to fruition and the time to spend designing and fine-tuning the board so that it is both attractive and easy to use. Because the rules of the game are not preestablished, they might also be more complicated for patrons to understand and remember as they progress through your program.

That said, game boards might be just the kind of gimmick required to engage reluctant participants. While reading and logging titles or checking off boxes on a bingo card might seem boring or mundane to these patrons, the idea of playing a game might just pique the interest of their competitive side and get them excited about summer reading. Another great benefit of the game board method is that participants can work at their own pace, selecting how and when to move forward and approaching milestones in their own time. Figure 2.3 shows a basic design for a game board to use for a teen summer reading program.

Checklist

If you like certain aspects of both the bingo approach and the game board approach, a checklist might be the ideal reporting tool for your summer reading program. It combines the simple look and straightforward rules of a bingo card with the flexibility and self-paced progression of the game board. To make a checklist, all you will need to do is make a list of summer reading tasks, arrange them in an eye-catching way in a document, and print the necessary number of copies. After your patrons check off the number of completed tasks you suggest, they report to you for their reward or recognition. The checklist is a good choice if you do not want to limit your patrons to just five tasks, as in the bingo board, or if you do not have the graphic design skills necessary to create a full game board. Figure 2.4 shows a sample checklist intended for use with a school-age summer reading program.

Calendar

If the goal of your summer reading program is to keep patrons reading all summer, and not just until they complete the requirements of an arbitrary challenge, a calendar is your

READ TO 100

This summer, make your way to 100 points by reading books and performing other book-related tasks. Here's how:

- Point values for each task are listed below.
- As you earn points, mark off boxes on the game board.
- When you reach 100 points, return your game board to the library to complete the challenge.

+20 Points
- Read a book, magazine, graphic novel, comic book, etc.
- Write a poem or short story.

+10 Points
- Attend a summer reading event.
- Create artwork inspired by something you have read.
- Volunteer 1 hour at the library.
- Complete the summer reading scavenger hunt.

+5 Points
- Write a book review.
- Read a poem, short story, or article.
- Read to someone else for 30 minutes.

1	2	3	4	5	6	7	8	9	10
11	12	13	14	15	16	17	18	19	20
21	22	23	24	25	26	27	28	29	30
31	32	33	34	35	36	37	38	39	40
41	42	43	44	45	46	47	48	49	50
51	52	53	54	55	56	57	58	59	60
61	62	63	64	65	66	67	68	69	70
71	72	73	74	75	76	77	78	79	80
81	82	83	84	85	86	87	88	89	90
91	92	93	94	95	96	97	98	99	100

Figure 2.3. Summer Reading Game Board for Teens. *Created by the author*

best bet for a reporting tool. With the calendar approach, you create a calendar that shows all the dates of your program, assigning one specific summer reading task to each date. You then challenge your patrons to check off a certain number of days to receive a prize. By focusing on daily participation instead of a set end goal, you help participants develop a regular reading habit and keep them connected to the library all summer long.

Another variation on the calendar approach is to distribute a new summer reading calendar at the start of each month rather than providing a single one for the entire summer. With this approach, you do not necessarily need to provide a task for each day. Instead, participants can complete a given month at their own pace; they just have to wait until the next month for the new set of tasks. Either way, patrons are involved with your program all summer and not just for a few days at the start of the season. Figure 2.5 is a basic calendar for prereading children that can be used as a template for designing your own.

Digital Software

Though pen-and-paper tracking methods are still popular in many communities, there is a growing shift toward using digital software for tracking summer reading progress. Digital tracking methods cut down on paperwork and recordkeeping for both patrons and librarians. They make it easy to sort, manage, and share summer reading data, and they integrate nicely with a library's existing web presence.

Summer Reading Challenge

Check off ten tasks below to complete the reading challenge!

- ❏ Read a fantasy or science fiction novel.
- ❏ Watch the film version of a book you have read.
- ❏ Reread an old favorite.
- ❏ Listen to an audiobook.
- ❏ Download and read an e-book.
- ❏ Read aloud to a family member or friend.
- ❏ Memorize a poem and recite it to a librarian.
- ❏ Design a new cover for a book you have read.
- ❏ Read a graphic novel.
- ❏ Do an art project inspired by a book you have read.
- ❏ Read a biography.
- ❏ Read a wordless book.
- ❏ Use a cookbook to prepare a dish.
- ❏ Attend a summer reading event.
- ❏ Attend a book club meeting.
- ❏ Read a book published before you were born.
- ❏ Read a book that won an award.
- ❏ Read a fairy tale or folk tale.
- ❏ Read a historical fiction novel.
- ❏ Write a book review.
- ❏ Read a play.

Figure 2.4. Summer Reading Checklist for School-Age Readers. *Created by the author*

SUMMER READING CALENDAR
for Prereaders

Here is your summer reading calendar for the month of July. Cross off each day as you complete its assigned task. At the end of the month, return the calendar to the library and pick up a new one for August!

1	2	3	4	5	6	7
Read a book about animals.	Sing a lullaby together.	Draw a picture of a book character.	Read from a poetry collection.	Sing or chant a nursery rhyme.	Look for the letters in your name on signs in your neighborhood.	Read a book about community helpers.
8	**9**	**10**	**11**	**12**	**13**	**14**
Draw a picture of your favorite nursery rhyme or fairy tale.	Sing the ABCs.	Read a book about the beach.	Read a nonfiction book.	Sing in the car or on the bus.	Color with crayons.	Read a children's magazine.
15	**16**	**17**	**18**	**19**	**20**	**21**
Read a book about space.	Read sitting beneath a tree.	Have a poetry picnic.	Read a book about dinosaurs.	Play I Spy to practice using describing words.	Read a book that was the childhood favorite of a grown-up you love.	Act out a favorite story.
22	**23**	**24**	**25**	**26**	**27**	**28**
Read a wordless picture book.	Make up a song.	Use a recipe to prepare a simple dish.	Play a guessing game.	Make an alphabet collage from old magazines and newspapers.	Read a book about kings and queens.	Read a rhyming book.
29	**30**	**31**				
Watch a video picture book.	Listen to an audiobook.	Make up a story about your family.				

Figure 2.5. Summer Reading Calendar for Early Childhood. *Created by the author*

Earlier in this chapter, table 2.1 listed software applications for registering summer reading participants for nondigital summer reading programs. Table 2.2, by contrast, shows the most commonly used web-based software programs that allow patrons to both register for and participate in a summer reading program online, along with the software's main features.

Reading Incentives

As your patrons track their reading and meet the goals established by your program, you might choose to reward their efforts with various reading incentives. This section will

Table 2.2. Web-Based Summer Reading Management Software Programs

METHOD	DESCRIPTION	FEATURES
Beanstack	A platform designed specifically for schools and libraries that host reading programs.	• Customizable design • Freedom to choose among program types and accompanying graphics • Manages registration for individuals and groups • Makes reports available on demand • Allows libraries to create booklists • Provides reading recommendations to patrons • Accessible on any device
Wandoo Reader	A game-like reading tracker provided by Evanced.	• One-step registration process • Family registration and management • Engages patrons with challenges, characters, points, etc. • Detailed reports • Accessible on mobile devices • Careful control over staff access
srp.Insight	Comprehensive summer reading program manager provided by LibraryInsight, Inc.	• Allows patrons to register and track titles read • Allows multiple simultaneous programs • Supports a Read-to-Me program for prereaders • Available in English and Spanish • Step-by-step guide for creating reading programs • Provides email communication with patrons • Supports libraries with single locations and multiple branches, as well as county systems • Allows use of CSS to customize design
RC App	Online solution for managing summer reading programs provided by Counting Opinions	• Annual subscription service • Unlimited number of reading programs • Embeds registration and tracking into library's website • Allows registration of individuals or groups • Provides end-of-summer survey for parents/caregivers
Readsquared	Reading program management tool that is an expanded version of the former Great Reading Adventure	• Customized programming • Advanced reporting • Mobile interface • Allows for collaboration with community organizations

help you decide how best to incorporate prizes into your summer reading program. Later chapters will address the particulars of selecting prizes for each different age group.

Tangible Prizes versus Experiential Prizes

Typically, summer reading incentives fall into two categories: tangible rewards (prizes that patrons take home and keep) and experiential rewards (opportunities to enjoy particular activities or events at the library or elsewhere in the community). Each of these types of prizes has advantages and disadvantages.

Tangible prizes can be appealing because their distribution requires little work from library staff. Patrons can stop by and ask for the prizes they have earned, and staff members can easily provide them within the context of typical daily library work. Tangible prizes can also serve as souvenirs of patrons' summer reading experiences, which is especially appealing to families with children. Material rewards can also help to market your library if they are branded with the library's logo and contact information.

Tangible prizes do present some challenges, however. If your community serves a large population or has limited storage space, it can be difficult to find a place to house your summer reading prizes prior to their distribution. If your library has a small budget for summer reading prizes, it can also be difficult to afford material rewards that are of high quality. This sometimes leads to libraries buying prizes of lesser quality in order to purchase the number required to meet the demand. Predicting demand is also difficult, and sometimes libraries wind up purchasing too many prizes, which exacerbates the storage problem, or too few, which disappoints many patrons.

The challenges associated with material prizes have led some libraries to begin offering more experiential rewards. The nice thing about experiential rewards is that you can be flexible and create a reward system that suits your library's specific needs and goals. In some libraries, experiential rewards are personalized for individuals. Children might be invited to have their photo taken wearing a crown, for example, or adult patrons may have the opportunity to have their name printed on a plate inside the cover of a particular book. Other libraries choose to offer a larger-scale experience, such as an ice cream party or the opportunity to see a librarian shave his head, which is shared by all recipients of the reward at once. Sometimes a library might even be able to partner with a local business or organization to provide an experiential prize. Examples might be allowing summer reading winners to visit the dugout of a local baseball team or providing a special film screening just for library summer reading participants.

Forgoing material prizes in favor of experiences also eliminates the problem of handing out "junk" prizes made of cheap materials that have little value for the patron. Because experiential rewards can be almost anything, you are much more likely to be able to find a high-quality reward that suits your budget and actually pleases your patrons as well.

Along with the advantages of flexibility and the elimination of low-quality rewards, however, come the drawbacks of experiential rewards. Providing special experiences as rewards for summer reading participation can mean a lot of work for librarians during a time of year that is already exceedingly busy. Even a single event at the end of the summer requires preparation and planning that is not necessary when you distribute material prizes. Experiential rewards are also dependent on the ability of patrons to come to the library at certain times. This is not as problematic with individualized experiences, as these can likely be provided on the spot, but if the experiential reward is an event scheduled for a specific date and time, it is basically guaranteed that not everyone who earns the prize will be able to enjoy it.

Benchmarks and Final Prizes

Whether you offer tangible or experiential rewards at your library, you will need to decide when during the summer reading program these are offered to your patrons. Generally, libraries approach this in one of two ways. Some prefer to chart patrons' progress throughout the summer by providing prizes when particular benchmarks are reached. These may include prizes offered at the time of registration, at the halfway point in the program, or at the end of each week or month of the summer reading program. Other libraries offer only one prize per patron, which is given upon completion of the summer reading program.

Benchmark prizes are not always necessary, but they can be helpful in keeping patrons invested in the program for the duration of the summer. Rewarding patrons for reaching particular benchmarks can also prevent patrons from simply finishing the entire program in a day or two. If patrons can receive several prizes throughout the summer, they may be more inclined to enjoy the program over the course of several weeks instead of rushing to finish just so they can have the prize.

When it comes to final prizes for completion of an entire summer reading program, there are two main schools of thought. In one camp are librarians who believe every participant in summer reading should be given a prize. In the other are those librarians who prefer to purchase larger, more expensive prizes with the understanding that only a few winners will be chosen by lottery or raffle. While it is ideal to validate the participation of every patron by offering a reward for each person's hard work, there are also ways to make the raffle concept more palatable and less confusing for patrons:

- Always mention the raffle any time you mention the associated prize. When patrons see an exciting summer reading prize, such as a bicycle or an e-reader, they can easily become caught up in their excitement and forget to read the fine print. To avoid disappointing patrons, especially kids and teens, you should make it clear in all promotional materials and in all interactions with patrons that these grand prizes will be awarded only to a certain number of participants, who will be chosen by lottery from those who have finished the summer reading program. When participants report to you that they have finished the summer reading program, remind them again that they are being entered into a raffle but are not guaranteed a prize.
- Offer a small token of recognition to all participants. Even when it is not feasible to offer a reward to every single individual patron, it is still a good idea to recognize each patron's participation in the summer reading program with a small token. This can be as simple as a certificate of completion bearing the patron's name and signed by the library director. Showing your appreciation for each participant's efforts can help lessen the disappointment felt by those patrons whose names are not selected during the raffle.
- Be open and clear about the lottery process. Even if your process for choosing prize winners is very basic, make sure to publicize how it will be handled. This includes stating who is eligible to win, when the prizes will be selected, and even who will do the drawing. (If you can enlist a staff member or other community member

who has no involvement with the summer reading program to draw the winners' names, it is a good idea to do so.) By making it clear how the raffle will unfold and then following that plan to the letter, you cut down on the number of patrons who become upset when they do not win.

⊚ Scheduling Summer Events

Though summer reading programs are first and foremost about encouraging and promoting reading, most libraries also offer events during the summer months to complement the summer reading program and encourage the community to visit the library. These events may include year-round activities that you wish to continue during the summer, performances by professional entertainers and educators, and special classes and activities connected to the summer reading theme. Figure 2.6 shows a professional performer giving a library presentation during a summer reading program.

Regardless of the exact type of activities you choose to offer in a given summer, you will need to consider the same key factors as you plan your schedule. First, you want to make sure you maximize the potential for each event's success by scheduling activities at times when you expect your target audience to be available. It is never a good practice to rely on an event to bring you an audience. If patrons typically do not attend evening events, for example, this is unlikely to change even if you have a really appealing evening event on the calendar. To avoid the frustration and embarrassment of having a low turn-out, or no audience at all, try to schedule events in time slots that have typically been

DO READING INCENTIVES WORK?

In recent years, some libraries have begun to eliminate incentives from their summer reading programs, citing research that shows that issuing prizes for reading does not always have the intended effect of motivating people—especially kids—to read. Studies have shown that extrinsic rewards actually contribute to a decline in a child's intrinsic desire to read. Children begin to believe they are reading not for the benefits brought about by books but for the promised prize and nothing more (Pressley and Allington, 2014). Even children who are already in the habit of reading lose some of their motivation when extrinsic rewards are available. In other words, the reward sets up a system in which the only reason to read is the prize. When a prize is not available, the desire to read dissipates.

In section 2 of *No More Reading for Junk*, Linda B. Gambrell identifies the true sources of individuals' motivation to read: access, relevance, and choice (Gambrell, 2016). These three elements are all connected to the reading material available to the children and not to any external reward system. As libraries already provide access to many relevant books and encourage children to freely choose their reading materials, they have already cornered the market on motivating kids to read. By eliminating prizes from their summer reading programs, libraries can truly capitalize on the opportunity they have to teach children and teens to enjoy reading for its own sake.

Figure 2.6. A professional magician performs at a library summer reading event. *Photo by Corporal Damien Gutierrez*

popular. Alternatively, schedule events at times when you have a group scheduled to visit the library. This alleviates the burden of having to create new activities just for the group and also guarantees an audience for events the general public might not be able to attend due to timing.

Similarly, be aware of the ways in which summer vacation may change the typical behavior of your library patrons. If you choose to offer a lot of the same programs in the summer as you do year-round, you may find that attendance changes dramatically during the summer months. In some circumstances, the number of attendees might increase exponentially, creating the need to require registration during the summer months for events that would not ordinarily require any gatekeeping. Conversely, if patrons are away on vacation or involved in scheduled activities at times that are different from when they are busy during the school year, you might see them lose interest in your established library programs during the summer months. Attendance statistics from past summers can help you make educated guesses about changes that might occur. Conducting a survey of your patrons—formally or informally—prior to the creation of your event schedule can also provide valuable information.

As you schedule summer events, also keep in mind the staffing levels you will have available to you in the summer. Will some staff members be on vacation during certain times? Are there days of the week where summer volunteers will be on site to assist with events? Will certain events require more staff to be present than would normally be scheduled on a typical day? Figuring out the logistics of your staff coverage will help you figure out which time slots are feasible for the events you would like to host and also allows you to discuss any needed scheduling changes with your supervisor.

As you plan your summer reading program, it can be helpful to have a timeline to follow to make sure that tasks are being completed in a timely fashion. Before you can use the timeline that appears below, however, you will need to determine a start date for your program. The launch of a summer reading program varies widely depending on location. In states where school lets out in May, summer reading can start as early as the first of May, while other states might end school in June, thus delaying the start of a summer reading program until June or even early July. Whenever you choose to start your program, you should always begin your preliminary planning around eight months ahead of the determined start date and definitely start setting things in stone no later than the start of the new year in January.

The timeline provided here purposely does not name specific months in order to accommodate the many differences among libraries, but it does give a rough idea of how

WORKING WITH SUMMER READING PERFORMERS

When you hire outside performers to make presentations at the library during your summer reading program, it is important to help make their events successful. To ensure a positive experience working with paid and volunteer performers, follow these rules of thumb:

1. Choose a performer wisely. Not all performers will suit your specific library's schedule, needs, or interests. Research your options carefully before deciding who to hire, and seek out references from other libraries. When selecting performers for children, consider the ages of the children who frequent your library and look for presenters who do programs tailored to their developmental needs. Consider holding a performer showcase early in the planning process so you can evaluate presenters' work firsthand.
2. Communicate. Performers who work with libraries generally know that spaces and equipment vary from location to location, but do not wait for them to ask you what is available or what you expect from them. Instead, lay out your expectations and policies when you first make contact and continue to communicate during the weeks and days leading up to the performance. Also find out from the performer if he or she will need anything from you on the day of the event. Performers may need to use a microphone, easel, or projector or require something as small as a pencil or a bottle of water. By discussing all these details ahead of time, you will make sure that both the library and the performer are prepared, thus contributing to a positive experience for everyone.
3. Staff the event. Even when a professional performer has been hired to make a presentation, the event itself is still being sponsored by the library and a representative of the library should be present. A librarian or other staff member should take responsibility for enforcing library policy during the event and for handling any last-minute questions or problems. Being present at the event

also allows you to observe the performer and the audience's reaction to him or her, which can be useful for future hiring decisions and for including anecdotes about summer reading in reports and newsletters.

4. Follow up after the presentation. After the conclusion of any paid or volunteer performance in your library, check in with your presenter. Thank him or her for the presentation, and share any positive feedback you received from patrons as they left the event. If there were any issues before or during the program, take a moment to discuss tactfully what went wrong and consider ways to improve the experience in the future. While you might be too busy to linger for long after the program, it is best not to let the performer simply walk out of the library without at least a brief moment to connect with him or her.

far ahead you need to plan in order to launch your program successfully at the appointed time. You may find it necessary to rearrange some items to suit your specific library's needs, but this template will provide you with a framework from which to work.

Eight Months Prior to Start Date

- Establish summer reading committee and create meeting schedule.
- Develop goals for the upcoming summer reading program.
- Decide whom your program will serve.
- Create a budget for the summer reading program.
- Reach out to potential donors for prizes and/or funding, including your Friends of the Library.

Seven Months Prior to Start Date

- Select a summer reading theme and order themed supplies.
- Begin researching performers you might like to hire and community groups who might be available to provide events and activities.

Six Months Prior to Start Date

- Establish registration method and reward system for your program.
- Order prizes and any other remaining supplies.

Five Months Prior to Start Date

- Hire and schedule all performers.
- Create first draft of schedule of all summer reading events.

Four Months Prior to Start Date

- Begin work on themed book lists.
- Make contact with camps and other groups who often book library visits in the summer to discuss scheduling.

Three Months Prior to Start Date

- Contact schools to schedule class visits.
- Finalize summer reading event schedule.
- Finalize book lists.

Two Months Prior to Start Date

- Print promotional materials and book lists.
- Begin publicizing your summer reading program in local media outlets.
- Contact all summer reading performers to go over details.
- Publish summer reading information online.

One Month Prior to Start Date

- Visit schools during their last few weeks of classes.
- Finalize all visits from camps and groups.
- Distribute promotional materials in-house.
- Share summer reading information on social media.

Upon Completion of Summer Reading

- Calculate participation statistics and report to administration.
- Distribute prizes.
- Have a summer reading committee meeting to critique the program. Record your comments for the next year's committee.

Following a planning schedule will help all staff members stay on the same page when it comes to summer reading planning, and it will ensure that no important task is left unfinished or left too late to finish well.

Key Points

This chapter has given you an overview of the key features of a successful summer reading program.

- Develop small, measurable goals to help guide your library's vision for each year's summer reading program.
- Use a summer reading theme to help you plan your program. Think flexibly about the theme for best results.
- Target your summer reading program toward the demographics that typically use your library.
- As you set up registration for your summer reading program, consider the advantages and disadvantages of paper-based and computer-based methods, and remember to request only the personal information you absolutely need.
- Great reporting tools for tracking patrons' summer reading progress include reading logs, bingo cards, game boards, checklists, calendars, and digital options.

- Reward patrons for their reading using tangible or experiential rewards. Choose whether to give prizes for reaching certain benchmarks or to give them only for completing the program.
- Use a planning timeline to help you accomplish all preparatory summer reading tasks in a timely manner.

Now that you have an understanding of the general framework for a summer reading program, the next few chapters will help you learn how to develop appropriate programs for specific age groups.

References

Gambrell, Linda B. 2016. "Why Not? What Works? What We Know about Reading Motivation and What It Means for Instruction." In *No More Reading for Junk* by Barbara A. Marinak and Linda B. Gambrell, 13–34. Portsmouth, NH: Heinemann.

Pressley, Michael, and Richard L. Allington. 2014. *Reading Instruction That Works: The Case for Balanced Teaching*. 4th ed. New York: Guilford Press.

CHAPTER 3

Summer Reading Programs for Early Childhood (Ages 0–5)

BABIES, TODDLERS, AND PRESCHOOLERS TYPICALLY do not know how to read, yet many libraries offer summer reading programs for this age range. This chapter will explain the reasons for providing summer reading programming for prereaders and discuss how to implement an effective and appealing early childhood program.

◉ Why Include Prereaders?

Traditionally, library summer reading programs have focused mainly on independent readers in the elementary grades who might experience summer learning loss if they do not read during their time off from school. Because children under five generally do not know how to read, it might seem counterintuitive to include them in the summer reading program, but there are actually very good reasons to do so.

The chief reason to offer early childhood summer reading programs is that literacy begins to develop from birth, right along with language. During the first five years of life, children benefit greatly from activities that help to promote early literacy skills. These skills, which have been identified by the Every Child Ready to Read initiative, are phonological awareness, phonemic awareness, narrative skills, letter knowledge, print awareness, and print motivation. The six skills have also been distilled into five easy-to-remember practices: singing, talking, reading, writing, and playing. Most libraries are already committed to supporting families as they help their children engage in these practices and acquire these skills, so it only makes sense to include those same children in the summer reading program. Because a summer reading program for young children encourages parents to read aloud to their prereaders and to engage in other early literacy–related activities, it can be a valuable motivator for families to work on developing a child's foundation in these early literacy skills.

Summer reading programs for early childhood also allow children the opportunity to learn to love the library from a very young age. Many libraries focus on developing a lifelong love of reading, so it only follows that they would want to engage children with library programs from birth. There is no guarantee that every prereader you serve in your summer reading program will grow to be a library user as a child, teen, or adult, but the chances of this happening are certainly greater when you have an early childhood program in place.

Finally, from a more practical standpoint, many families really like programs that invite participation from every member of the family. It can be difficult to leave out a younger sibling, for example, while older kids enjoy their own reading program. By offering a program for your youngest patrons, you eliminate a potential roadblock that might prevent some families from participating in summer reading at all.

◉ Convincing Caregivers to Participate

Patrons with young children are often very busy, and their trips to the library may be sporadic occurrences that fit into their schedules among many other activities and appointments. To these busy parents and caregivers, the notion of an early childhood summer reading program might seem like yet another overwhelming, burdensome task to add to their ever-growing list of obligations. To combat this, the librarian should make the program as appealing as possible. There are several ways to accomplish this.

Develop an Appropriately Challenging Program

Summer reading is especially appealing to parents and caregivers when it is a little bit demanding but not too difficult to add to their busy routines. To make sure you are striking the right balance, do your best to make your program something that takes all summer rather than a quick and easy task that can be completed in only a day or two. Examples might be challenging parents to read to their children under five for fifteen minutes a day, five days a week or asking participants to check off a certain number of reading-related activities on a monthly calendar. Programs that use these formats feel more relaxed because patrons have the flexibility to choose when they participate, and there is no penalty for missing a few days here and there. They also feel more worthwhile because they give children an activity that lasts all summer in which they and their families can become invested.

Caregivers do not want to be overwhelmed with a program that feels impossible to complete, but they also do not want to participate in busywork instead of an activity with real value for their families. If your program appears as though it will help families develop strong reading habits with their young children, it will appeal much more to most caregivers than a program that looks like nothing more than a means to earning a prize or a bone thrown to prereaders.

Make Your Program Sound Fun

Sometimes librarians get so caught up in proving to parents that reading to their children is important and educational that they forget to also point out how much fun it is. While you should certainly make your patrons aware of the benefits of reading with their kids, it is equally important to emphasize the intrinsic value in reading as a family simply for the enjoyment it brings.

In order to make summer reading sound fun, avoid including a lot of early literacy jargon on your promotional materials. A reference or two to the academic benefits of reading with young children is fine, but try not to give caregivers the impression that signing up for summer reading is the equivalent of enrolling their child in preschool. If the program sounds too academic, many parents who might otherwise be interested may assume they do not have the time or the room in their schedules and may decide not to sign up.

Provide Clear Instructions

Many parents tend to be turned off by programs with overly complicated rules and methods. This is not because they do not care enough about the program to decipher the instructions; it is more likely because they do not have a lot of extra time to spend jumping through hoops for the sake of something that is meant to be a fun part of their summer. Children may also be involved in multiple summer activities, so having to remember the intricacies of a summer reading program along with schedules for swim lessons and camp classes can quickly come to feel like a burden.

Truly parent-friendly summer reading instructions should get right to the point. If you cannot summarize the basics of your program in a few concise bullet points, then your program is probably more complicated than necessary and not as likely to entice parents and caregivers. Simplifying your program until you can convey all the pertinent information in just a few short sentences will go a long way toward encouraging caregivers to register their young children.

Avoid Being Pushy

It can be very discouraging when a caregiver has listened to your pitch for summer reading and chooses not to participate, but this is ultimately his or her prerogative and it should be respected. No matter how wonderful your program, there will always be some people who just will not want to be a part of it. It can be tempting to speculate about the motives of such patrons and to label them as difficult or even neglectful, but this is a waste of energy and an unprofessional approach. The role of the library is to offer programs for the community, and it is then up to community members to decide whether the specific offerings suit their personal needs.

Despite the strong urge you might have to continue arguing with a patron whom you would really like to convince to participate in summer reading, it is important to know when to let it go. If you do not push too hard, there is always at least a small chance that your patron will go home and think about what you have said and come back at a later time to sign up. If you become a nuisance to the patron, however, you might cause him or her to lose interest in the library altogether when previously the patron was only turned off by one specific program.

Ultimately, if you can demonstrate to parents that you understand what is important to them, and what works for them, they will be more likely to both register their young children for summer reading and participate throughout the program.

Selecting a Program Format

At this early stage of life, children can benefit most from developing a consistent daily reading habit. Though it might be tempting to make your program competitive by asking families to read for a certain amount of time or to reach an arbitrary total of books read, this is not the best approach. If the goal of the program is to have children exposed to books daily, then the challenge presented to families should really be just that simple: read every day and, possibly, receive a reward. Simplifying the program in this way makes it very easy for families to participate since there are no complicated requirements to remember, and it also helps you develop a reporting method for patrons to use. (Almost any of the reporting methods mentioned in chapter 2, "Developing a Summer Reading Program," can be used for an early childhood program.)

If your library is especially interested in promoting the six early literacy skills (phonological awareness, phonemic awareness, narrative skills, vocabulary, print awareness, and print motivation) or their five accompanying practices (sing, talk, read, write, and play), you can also supplement your summer reading program with specific challenges that support this type of learning. If you do this, however, make sure that the activities you include do truly connect in some way to literacy and that if the connection is not apparent, you make the connection for the patron in your printed instructions. Activities such as blowing bubbles, locating the local fire station, and swinging on a swing are all perfectly fun for kids in this age group, but none of these is an activity that inherently promotes early literacy skills. To make them truly appropriate as early literacy activities, you would have to enhance them so that perhaps you discuss the sizes of the bubbles as they appear, read a book in preparation for meeting a firefighter, or sing songs about flying while enjoying the swing. By explicitly stating the early literacy component for each activity, you keep the emphasis of the program on reading and avoid losing your focus on developing good reading habits in your young patrons. It is also important to remember that while play is an early literacy skill, not all forms of play promote literacy, and it is not necessary to link all play to a skill-building agenda.

Any early literacy activities that you choose to include in your summer reading program should also be things that a child in this age range is capable of doing or at least participating in. The best way to accomplish this is to leave each task as open-ended as possible. Instead of prompting children to write the alphabet with a pencil, for example, suggest that they practice writing using a crayon or pencil. Writing the alphabet may only be possible for some of the four- and five-year-olds, whereas nearly every child in this age range can hold a crayon or pencil and attempt to make a mark. By providing general activities, you allow families to judge how their child is best able to complete them, and you avoid frustrating parents and caregivers who might end up just doing the more difficult tasks themselves while the child passively observes. Here are some more types of suitable early literacy tasks to be included in your summer reading program:

- Singing songs related to the summer theme, daily activities, or particular books
- Reading stories in unusual places, such as the park, the pool, the car, on the beach, and so on
- Experimenting with chalk, crayons, pencils, and/or markers
- Describing objects in terms of size, color, shape, and number
- Reading books from a particular genre or section of the library
- Hunting for specific letters on the page of a book or for words beginning with that letter in the child's immediate environment
- Reciting or listening to nursery rhymes and poems

Prizes for Prereaders

Chapter 2, "Developing a Summer Reading Program," provided some basic information to help you decide whether and how to include incentives in your summer reading program. Assuming you have chosen to reward your early childhood participants with either tangible or experiential prizes, this section provides suggestions of age-appropriate rewards in both categories.

Tangible rewards for young children should be safe for their use and developmentally appropriate. Toys with small parts, anything sharp or likely to cause injury, or anything breakable are generally not good prizes for children under five. Developmentally, there is a wide range of capability during the first five years of life, so in situations where a single prize to satisfy every age within this bracket cannot be found, it might be appropriate to offer a separate prize for babies and toddlers than what is given to preschoolers. Regardless of what you choose, it should be of good quality and of good practical use to the child, either as a toy or as an everyday object to be used in their daily routines.

Examples of suitable tangible prizes for children ages zero to five are

- Board books or picture books
- Placemats
- Bibs (for babies)
- Rubber ducks or other rubber animals
- Crayons
- Bubbles
- Book bags

- Flashcards for learning the alphabet
- Sippy cups
- Small stuffed animals
- Soft balls

As your budget allows, you can order these items with your library's logo or your chosen consortium's themed summer reading artwork. Many of these prizes can also be ordered in bulk from suppliers such as Discount School Supply and Oriental Trading.

If you choose to avoid tangible items altogether but still want to reward your participants, you can offer an experiential prize. Kids in the early childhood age bracket generally do not have high expectations about summer reading prizes, so you do not have to offer something outrageous to make an impression. Thinking small will steer you in the right direction. Potential experiential rewards for ages zero to five include

- Adding the child's name to a bulletin board or display
- Taking the child's photo with a special prop, background, or hat
- Attending a special story time celebrating summer reading participants
- Providing coupons for a visit to a local zoo, museum, or other venue that caters to young children
- An end-of-summer concert with family-friendly musical performers
- A visit with a favorite character or local team mascot

Keep in mind that not all children will understand the significance of their rewards, particularly if they are under the age of two or new to the summer reading experience. Expect that some children will refuse their reward or claim not to like it and know that this is normal behavior during early childhood. Often children who seem less than enthusiastic about their prize at first will warm up to it when they leave the library, and others will have enjoyed the experience of participating more than the end result, which is definitely a positive outcome. To make families feel more comfortable, it can be beneficial to make them aware that it is acceptable to opt out of a reward. A simple sentence or two letting patrons know it is okay to turn down their prize should be sufficient. In figure 3.1, a group of preschool children reacts to receiving bags of toys as summer reading prizes.

Building Summer Book Lists for Prereaders

Building summer reading book lists for younger children is usually a task left to librarians rather than the school system, as most schools rightfully do not have summer reading requirements for children in preschool. When you create book lists for this age, it is wise to compile titles according to theme rather than according to the intended age group. Since children enrolled in the early childhood program will be hearing the books read aloud and generally not reading books to themselves, an age guideline on their book lists can only create anxiety and frustration for parents who might be worried about their young children's reading abilities or lack thereof. If there are schools and daycares in the community with whom you have strong relationships, do feel free to ask for their input when making these lists, but make it clear that you are not seeking to give the children an academic task. As you come up with your own selections and take suggestions, also make sure you are including a mix of picture books, board books, and age-appropriate nonfic-

Figure 3.1. Preschoolers receive bags of toys during a "Read to the Rhythm" summer reading event. *U.S. Air Force photo by Senior Airman Ty-Rico Lea*

tion so that you give equal attention to each area of your collection. Also be mindful of including formats other than traditional print books, including any e-books, audiobooks, or related DVDs you may have in your collection.

Some summer reading themes lend themselves better to certain age groups than others, and there will be years where if you are using a theme, you might feel lost when it comes to promoting books to your youngest readers. When this occurs, it is helpful to think broadly about the theme and stretch it as far as you can to make it work. For example, in 2016 the Collaborative Summer Library Program (CSLP) theme was On Your Mark, Get Set, Read! and early in the planning process, many librarians struggled to find suitable sports-themed books for babies and toddlers. However, they ultimately found ways to mold the theme to suit their purposes, stretching sports and fitness to include healthy eating, outdoor play, making friends, and other topics that were friendlier to early childhood. This is another instance where it is also helpful to remember that reading is always a part of the summer reading theme, and any book you suggest certainly promotes that.

Ultimately, book lists for this age group are really just tools to help parents navigate your library's collection. In addition to lists specifically tailored to the summer's chosen theme, it is also a good idea to have copies available of book lists on perennially popular themes, such as transportation, animals, princesses, counting books, and so on. If you have these lists available in your library year-round, there may not even be a need to create new ones at all, as long as you have enough copies available to serve the number of patrons you expect to see in the summer.

⑥ Offering Story Times during Summer Reading

Along with reading, completing early literacy tasks, and earning rewards, families of children in the early childhood age group also enjoy attending story time during the summer months. Because summer reading is a huge, time-consuming endeavor, some libraries choose to discontinue story time during the summer in order to alleviate some of the demands on their staff. While it is understandable why a library might choose to do this, it is really not an ideal practice. If at all possible, it is best to continue offering story time in some format even while your summer reading program is happening.

Reasons to Offer Summer Story Times

There are several reasons to offer summer story times. First, cancelling story time for the summer reading program is very inconvenient and disappointing to many families. It is true that summer is a very different time of year for the library and for children and teens who attend school, so it might seem like taking this time off from the regular routine of the school year is something everyone can understand. For families whose children do not yet attend school, however, summer is much the same as other seasons, except that the weather is often nicer for going out with babies and toddlers than it is during the rest of the year. By not offering story time in the summer, you lose your opportunity to interact with families who cannot come to story time the rest of the year or who count on story time to keep their children engaged in a regular productive activity.

A second major reason to offer story time in the summer is that it gives you a platform for promoting summer reading and an added incentive for summer reading participants to visit the library regularly. Since many of the early childhood patrons whose families would be interested in summer reading are likely to be regular story time attendees, you do not want to potentially alienate this audience by cancelling their favorite activity just as your summer reading program begins. If your story time is going strong, it makes sense to stick with it and to make it a priority during the summer months.

Finally, continuing story times through the summer is easier on librarians than having to develop brand-new activities to complement the summer reading program. While it can be fun to change things up a little bit during the summer, this can be done just as well within the context of story time as it can be by reinventing your entire event schedule. Instead of abandoning story time in favor of supposedly more engaging programming, consider combining story time with other special activities like playtime, sing-alongs, or a dance party. Not only does this make the story times feel more special during a special time of year, but it also reduces the amount of planning you must do if half of your story time is devoted to an unstructured summer activity.

Planning Summer Story Times

As you consider how best to incorporate story times into your summer reading program, there are several factors on which you should focus your attention:

- The number of story times you offer. While it is ideal to offer story time during the summer, this does not automatically mean that you must offer your full story time schedule while summer reading is going on. It is definitely reasonable to make changes to your story time schedule to accommodate the busier summer months, and in general your patrons will appreciate your efforts. If you are in the habit of offering separate weekly story times for each of several age groups, consider cutting that down to just one family or all-ages story time each week. If space is a problem, limit attendance using tickets or registration or try holding the story time outdoors, where there is more room for larger groups. This way if there are multiple story time providers on your staff, you can take turns offering story time each week, thereby cutting down on everyone's planning time. Offering fewer story times also frees up some time slots in your schedule for summer reading performances and other special events.

- The content of your story time. As mentioned in the last section, it is possible to combine other special activities with your story times in order to create variety and reduce the amount of structured planning you must do. Another option is to plan more repetitive content. Instead of planning a new story time from scratch each week, you could use a nearly identical framework for each session—same rhymes, same songs, same stretches—and just choose different books from week to week. While selecting books will take up some of your time, it will be significantly less than the time you would spend planning an entire story time from start to finish. While your audience might notice this new approach, they will be unlikely to complain. Kids thrive on repetition, and their caregivers might appreciate the chance to learn a core group of songs and rhymes really well.

- The summer reading theme. If your library is using a theme for your summer reading program, you will need to decide whether, how, and when to use the theme for your story times. If you never use themes at story time, it might not even occur to you to use the summer theme to inform your story time content, and that is not a problem. If you are someone who thrives on themes, however, you might wonder whether there is enough story time content on the chosen theme to sustain an entire summer's worth of story times, and if there is not, you might wonder what you should do. The fact is that most of your summer reading participants in this age group are not even going to notice if every story time matches the theme. Let yourself off the hook and do only what you can manage. Some librarians choose to present a single story time connected to the summer theme at the start of the summer and then abandon the theme entirely in favor of unrelated themes or no theme at all. Others make it a point to brainstorm topics connected with the theme and offer story times centered on those ideas even if they are only tangentially related to the main focus of summer reading. Still others use story time to promote the reading aspect of each theme and never worry about making a direct connection to the specific topic assigned to a given summer. Each of these approaches works very well, and your choice is really just a matter of personal preference.

- Potential changes in attendance. Depending on the summer habits of your community, you might see a volatile change in your story time attendance. This could be an increase or decrease in the number of attendees, a change in the average age of attendees, and even a sudden preference among your patrons for a different day or time slot. If you have observed the trends in your library during the summer months in the past, these can inform your decisions about summer story times. In some cases, you may discover that using a modified version of your year-round schedule works fine; in others, you may suddenly find yourself offering afternoon, evening, and weekend story times you would never think to include on your calendar in other seasons. As you plan, be prepared to think outside the box to accommodate the community changes sometimes associated with summer vacation.

In addition to story times, many libraries like to offer special events for early childhood summer reading participants. This section provides a selection of tried-and-true activities for this age group that can be adapted to suit any summer reading theme and therefore can be used year after year with only minor adjustments.

StoryWalk

A StoryWalk is an outdoor activity where children and caregivers read a picture book by walking together from page to page. Because a StoryWalk is meant to be held outdoors, it is a perfect summer event. The original program was created by Anne Ferguson of Montpelier, Vermont, and developed in collaboration with the Vermont Bicycle & Pedestrian Coalition and the Kellogg Hubbard Library, and it is coordinated by Let's Go!, an obesity prevention program of the Barbara Bush Children's Hospital at Maine Medical Center. StoryWalk is a registered trademark, so if you choose to hold one at your library using the guidelines provided by the Kellogg Hubbard Library, you must call the event a StoryWalk, and you must also post a disclaimer that gives proper credit to the founder of the program and states that she has registered StoryWalk as a trademark. Many libraries have also adopted the idea as their own under slightly different titles.

Whether your event is an official StoryWalk, a "story book walk," or a "story time stroll," you will need the same basic supplies: two copies of the book you would like to use, a means of weatherproofing the pages, and wooden stakes for mounting the pages and assembling the story outdoors. A third copy of the book and replacement stakes may also be necessary if your StoryWalk is to be available over a long period of time, such as the entire summer, as this will make it easy to repair or replace particular pages of the story as needed. You might also want to include a notebook and pencil at the start or end of the walk so that users can record their participation and you can keep accurate statistics of how the StoryWalk is being used.

To put together the story, take apart the two copies of the book and laminate each page or two-page spread. Make sure you have one copy of each page or spread, and then attach each one to a stake. In an outdoor space that is large enough to accommodate at least a few families at a time, arrange the stakes in the correct order. Libraries have placed their StoryWalks in lawns and gardens surrounding their buildings, as well as in local parks and on nature trails in their communities. In smaller spaces, even the front walk of the library or the perimeter of the parking lot can work. Wherever you set up, make sure you can leave at least some space between pages so that different participants can look at separate pieces of the story simultaneously without crowding each other and so that the physical-activity element of the program is not lost. When the StoryWalk is fully assembled, walk through it yourself and make sure all pages are accounted for and posted in the correct order and that participants will easily understand which route to take as they make their way through the story.

Adapting this activity to your summer reading theme is as simple as choosing a book that connects to the topic. In years where your theme is about the outdoors, sports, or nature, the StoryWalk itself connects to the theme with no modifications at all. Also, because reading is always an element of the summer reading program, a StoryWalk is always an appropriate addition.

Stuffed Animal Sleepover

A stuffed animal sleepover is typically geared toward the preschool set (ages three to five). This is an evening event where children come to the library with their stuffed animals, do a few activities, and then leave the animals to "sleep" at the library. Once the children have gone home, librarians stage various scenes and photograph the stuffed animals making mischief and having fun at the library. The next day, the children return to the library to retrieve their stuffed friends and receive some of the photos as souvenirs.

Because this event only really requires three things to be successful—a camera, a group of children, and the children's stuffed animals—it is easy to adapt it for the summer reading theme with just a few embellishments. Here are just some of the ways you can coordinate your stuffed animal sleepover with a theme:

- Story time. Before the children leave for the night, have them attend a summer reading–themed story time with their stuffed animals. Include books, songs, and rhymes that connect in some way to the summer reading theme.
- Decorations. Decorate the space where the stuffed animals will spend the night with festive items related to the theme. This could be as simple as a display of library materials and as elaborate as streamers, balloons, and/or posters.
- Crafts and games. If the kids are going to do crafts or play games with their stuffed animals before leaving them for the night, see if you can find some that will connect with the summer theme and include those in your event.
- Music. Play some music related to the summer reading theme in the background as the kids participate in activities. If there is a lullaby related to the theme, teach the children to sing it to their stuffed animals.
- Photo props. As you photograph the stuffed animals, consider any props you have on hand that will connect to the theme. For an "around the world" theme, for example, a globe could be a useful prop, whereas the kitchen sink would work well for water, and an outdoor garden matches up nicely with a digging, growing, or gardening theme.

Once you establish your own routine for hosting a stuffed animal sleepover, it can easily become a summer tradition at your library. By simply adding a few slightly different thematic elements each year, you can vary the program slightly for variety without sacrificing a lot of extra time in planning and preparation.

Early Literacy Fair

At an early literacy fair, the library and other partner organizations that serve families with young children set up tables and booths to help promote early literacy skills to the public. The event can take place indoors or outdoors, and it can be as large scale or simple as your library can manage. Booths can include almost anything related to literacy that will engage small children and their caregivers. Some suggestions for activities are

- Allowing children to register for summer reading
- Giving away free board books or picture books
- Playing simple early literacy games
- Presenting story times

- Making alphabet-themed crafts
- Singing songs and/or playing a concert on a musical instrument
- Reciting poetry or nursery rhymes

Tailoring your fair to a theme involves choosing games, crafts, songs, and poems connected to the topic on which your summer reading program will focus. Because this is an event that can involve many community groups, it may gain more publicity than other summer events you offer. Therefore, it is a great event to host early in the summer as a kickoff to your reading program. Alternatively, a fair like this can make a great ending to a summer reading program and a segue into preschool.

Tea Parties

Tea parties can be held in celebration of a particular book, character, or genre, or they can have a more general focus on a topic connected to the summer reading theme. Since snacks are involved, tea parties are generally best for preschoolers and older toddlers who can eat solid food and drink from tea cups.

To host a tea party at your library, you will need a space large enough to host at least several families and a beverage to serve. Since children are not always fond of tea, libraries often have lemonade, punch, or juice instead. To accompany the tea, provide a few snacks. Fruits and vegetables, cookies, cheese and crackers, and small sandwiches are all appropriate choices, depending on the preferences of your community and any allergies the children may have.

You can decorate your tea party as simply or as elaborately as you would like. To add some thematic elements to the event, consider purchasing tablecloths, napkins, and paper cups bearing designs related to your theme. Balloons, vases of flowers, streamers, and other typical party decorations can also be selected in particular colors that suit the focus of the party and can be arranged throughout the party space. You can also give out party favors bearing the summer reading logo and the library's contact information.

In terms of activities, simple, age-appropriate games are best, especially those with an early literacy component. These can include basic scavenger hunts, bingo games, and guessing games, as well as circle games like the Farmer in the Dell and London Bridge Is Falling Down. If your summer reading program challenges kids to complete certain early literacy activities, you could also make some of these part of your tea party in order to encourage families to complete them.

Miscellaneous Unstructured Activities

In addition to these specific structured activities, there are lots of easy-to-plan unstructured events libraries offer year-round that also fit well into the summer reading program. These include dance parties, sing-alongs, playing with toys, building with LEGO® blocks, creating open-ended arts and crafts projects, and watching films. Adding just a few thematic elements to any of these events breathes new life into them and makes them feel new for your summer reading participants. Even just giving the event a themed title can sometimes be enough to entice new patrons to participate. For example, if the theme was "Dig into Reading," it would be fitting to name an event "Dig into Dancing" or "Dig into Painting," while a program titled "One World, Many Stories" lends itself well to things like "One World, Many Dances" or "One World, Many Songs." Considering all aspects of the theme and looking for ways to combine those aspects with activities you already offer will make it much easier for you to plan special summer reading events without spending all of your work time putting them together.

🌀 Key Points

This chapter has explored some of the special considerations you will want to make when planning a summer reading program for participants in the early childhood age range.

- Offering a summer reading program for prereaders helps promote early literacy skills and makes it more appealing and manageable for families to participate in summer reading overall.
- To entice caregivers to register their children for summer reading, develop an appealing and appropriately challenging program, provide straightforward instructions, and avoid placing undue pressure on families to participate.
- The best format for an early childhood summer reading program allows the program to last all summer and includes activities that children are developmentally capable of completing independently or with limited support from caregivers.
- Tangible summer reading rewards for young children should be safe and developmentally appropriate, have a practical use, and be unlikely to break. Experiential rewards need not be complicated to make a strong impression.
- Summer reading book lists for prereaders should include suggested titles from different areas of your collection and should be used primarily as a means of navigating the library's collection, not as an academic assignment.
- Make it easier for your library to offer story time during the summer months by making changes to your story time schedule and dividing the workload more equitably among staff members.
- Add elements connected to the summer theme to basic library activities in order to offer special events during summer reading without overtaxing your resources.

Now that you know how to serve prereaders during the summer reading program, the next chapter will help you begin to understand the needs of independent readers ages six to twelve.

CHAPTER 4

Summer Reading Programs for School-Age Children (Ages 6–12)

TRADITIONALLY, SUMMER READING PROGRAMS have been geared toward school-age children who can read independently. Members of this age bracket need solid reading skills to be able to achieve academically, and library summer reading programs have a long history of supporting these readers through the summer months in order to prevent learning loss. This chapter will focus on the special considerations libraries need to make when developing a summer reading program for the school-age population.

Leveling the Playing Field

The elementary years see children through an enormous amount of development in a relatively short period of time. At the younger end of this age range, there are very young children who have just begun to read independently. These children typically read short books of less than one hundred pages with many illustrations sprinkled throughout the text. At the higher end of the spectrum are preteens. Some of these children might be struggling readers who still read shorter, simpler titles, but many others are established readers with an affinity for lengthier novels of two hundred pages or more. The differences in ability and in the reading material itself make it difficult for all kids in the school-age program to compete against one another without giving an unfair advantage to one age group over another. As you determine how you will challenge your school-age participants to read regularly, it is important to look for ways to level the playing field among readers of highly disparate abilities.

One way some libraries try to ensure that no certain segment of the school-age population is given an unfair advantage is to break the group down into smaller segments based on age or grade level. Some do this by offering separate programs for beginning readers and fluent readers. Others may break the group down even further, even to the point of having a different program for every single age within this range. This does solve the problem for kids who are reading at or above grade level, but it can still pose a problem for struggling readers. How, for example, would a fifth grader who is still reading illustrated chapter books for beginners participate? Would that fifth grader be categorized as a beginning reader while the student's friends compete in the intermediate program, or would the student compete against others in the same age group, reading twice as many books as they do in the same amount of time because this particular student's books are shorter? Breaking the groups down in this way can sometimes have the opposite effect of what is intended, causing more difficulties in keeping things fair instead of promoting equality across the board.

An easier way to handle the problem of potential unfairness in your summer reading program is to have your readers keep track of their progress not by the number of books or pages they read but by how much time they spend reading. You could issue a challenge to read for a set number of minutes each day, week, or month or set a long-range goal for the entire summer. Asking kids to use time as a measuring tool accounts not only for the differences in reading abilities but also for the speed with which a child reads and for the length and format of the books he or she chooses. Tracking reading by time makes it possible for a child reading Shakespeare to compete fairly with a child still working on mastering Frog and Toad.

An alternative to tracking progress by time that has the same overall effect would be to use a checklist or bingo card to issue specific reading challenges to school-age readers. (These are described in chapter 2, "Developing a Summer Reading Program"). These types of tracking methods allow readers to choose reading material that both suits their capabilities and fulfills the given challenge. For example, a bingo card might list different genres but no specific titles. Readers could then choose a title in each genre that is also at their own reading level.

Finally, another easy way to level the playing field is to eliminate competition from your program altogether. Instead of having kids try to out-read their friends, have them select their own reading goal for the summer (perhaps with the help of a librarian, parent, or teacher), and reward them if and when they achieve it. Some kids might try to set a goal that is too low in order to make the program easier to complete, but these are likely to be the exception. Most kids take these personal goals seriously and work just as hard to compete with themselves as they would to compete against their peers.

Most of the time, parents remember participating in school-age summer reading programs during their own childhoods, so it is easier to convince them to have their kids participate at this stage than during either the early childhood or teen years. Parents are also frequently concerned about their children's reading progress, and pressure from local schools to keep their kids reading over the summer is another strong motivator in encouraging parents to register their kids for summer reading.

That said, you do not want to take this age group for granted. There are other summer reading programs available through booksellers like Barnes & Noble, restaurants like Chipotle and Pizza Hut, and other businesses that families may turn to if they are not satisfied with the library's program. To ensure that the school-age population, which has been the anchor of summer reading programs for decades, continues to participate in your program, pay careful attention to how you handle the following:

- Recordkeeping. Parents with school-age kids often come to the library laden down with paperwork related to their children's summer reading assignments from school. For some parents who are already juggling several school reading logs, the thought of having to handle another one can be overwhelming. To avoid upsetting a parent with the burden of yet another piece of paper to keep track of, consider allowing kids to photocopy their school log and turn it in for credit toward the library's summer reading program. This is a great way to show parents that you are truly trying to facilitate the goals they want their children to reach during the summer and that you are not hung up on red tape and paperwork.
- Technology. Incorporating technology into your summer reading program for school-age kids can be a help or a hindrance depending on your patrons. For patrons who have access to an Internet connection and compatible devices at home, a digital tracking method might be the ideal way for them to track their reading progress. A child can easily log in from home using a computer, tablet, or smartphone and update his or her reading progress as often the child wishes. For some kids, being able to see their progress in real time each day, perhaps with the occasional reward of a fun digital badge, can be a strong motivator to keep reading all summer. For families who do not have these luxuries at home, however, it can become burdensome to either keep track of everything on paper until they can visit the library or to visit the library several times a week to update their progress. If you have a patron base where many do not have access to the Internet from home, it might be best to either avoid a technology-based program or to have an alternative for families who would prefer not to use the web-based tracking method.
- Reading levels. It is widely understood among librarians that the reading levels attached to children's books are often flawed, misleading, and off-putting. For parents who are attempting to help their children fulfill school assignments, however, knowing the librarian's view on reading levels is not helpful. The fact is, many schools use reading levels to determine what kids should and should not be reading, and librarians need to be prepared to help parents navigate their collections to find books at particular levels. This is not to suggest that libraries ought to organize their collections according to reading level or even that librarians should direct kids only

to books on their predetermined level. It simply means that librarians should equip themselves to be able to assist parents in finding books based on their levels in common leveling systems such as Lexile, Renaissance Accelerated Reader, and the Fountas & Pinnell Benchmark Assessment Systems (commonly known as Guided Reading). If the library does not provide this service, even if only upon request, parents may find it necessary to find their children's summer reading material elsewhere and to avoid the library program altogether.

- Design of promotional materials. Though kids might be excited by the fact that their school assignments count toward the library's summer reading program or that there are digital badges available as rewards for reaching their reading goals, neither of these is enough on its own to entice a child to participate. Instead, it is the overall design of your program's promotional materials—flyers, signs, posters, and so on—that will encourage kids to find out more about what you can offer them. Brightly colored graphics, upbeat language, and simple, conversational explanations of instructions are all great ways to engage kids and get them excited about participating in summer reading. Even kids who are not especially enthusiastic readers can become excited about summer reading if the program is carefully tailored to their particular developmental needs and interests. While it is important to engage parents with your program's offerings, the program runs a lot smoother when kids themselves buy into it as well.

Prizes for School-Age Participants

Assuming that your summer reading program will award children with either tangible or experiential prizes, this section will cover some best practices for selecting and distributing these rewards.

The first rule of thumb when working with the school-age population is to ensure recognition for every child. Children in this age group are still very much developing as readers, and rewards for effort are as important as rewards for successfully completing a full program. If prizes are only awarded to a few readers, many kids who feel they have no chance of being a prizewinner might not put in that much effort or might simply sit out of the program altogether. If there is hope of winning even a small token of recognition, however, kids will be more inclined to feel that they can achieve success. It is fine to offer large rewards for kids who are selected from a raffle or for those who read the most, but to offer nothing for other participants makes kids feel that the program is only for certain select kids and not necessarily for everyone.

Likewise, rewards do not have to be overly expensive or flashy to be meaningful. Kids are often happy with simple items, such as stickers, pencils, small stuffed animals, and other library-branded giveaway items. Allowing kids to choose from a prize box or to win tickets for use in a prize store at the library is more than enough to satisfy most summer readers. Though it can create great opportunities for publicity when your library gives away bicycles, laptops, e-readers, tablets, and other large prizes, it also puts you in a situation where you are constantly trying to provide an even more exciting prize each year. This can become expensive, and it can make it feel impossible to ever change your prize-giving structure if you someday no longer wanted to give away big-ticket items. There is no need to be extravagant for the sake of giving a big prize to a small handful of children when that money could be spent to provide smaller prizes for every child. Examples of small, tangible prizes that appeal to school-age kids include

- Plastic bracelets
- Paper dolls
- Finger puppets
- Small puzzles
- Candy
- Paperback books
- Silly putty
- Blow-up toys such as beach balls
- Sunglasses
- Rubber or plastic figurines
- Erasers
- Pencil sharpeners
- Craft kits
- Watercolor paint boxes
- Trading cards
- Colorful shoelaces
- Certificates of completion

If your library prefers to reward summer reading participants without having to invest in cheap plastic toys, there are also a variety of experiential rewards that are appropriate for school-age kids. These can come in the form of events, such as an ice cream social, pizza party, or end-of-summer barbecue, or a family concert, film screening, or author visit. These can be open to all summer reading participants or, if space is an issue, available by invitation to those who finish the program.

There is also the possibility of having kids add their own personal touches to a communal bulletin board or display. Children can be invited to add their name, a drawing, a sticker, or some other small piece to a larger picture each time they finish a book or meet a set milestone in your program. Other options include

- Photos with a special prop or mascot
- The chance to act as "librarian for a day"
- Tickets to a special sporting event for summer reading participants
- Recognition in the library newsletter or on the library website
- Coupons for local zoos, museums, restaurants, attractions, and so on

⊚ Creating Book Lists

Creating book lists for the school-age summer reading program is an important task that libraries should never overlook. Though many school districts now provide extensive summer reading lists for their school-age students, these are often unique to the interests of particular teachers or administrators or designed by a school representative who is unfamiliar with the nuances of the public library's collection. To ensure that your summer reading participants are able to find reading material they will enjoy on the shelves at your library, it is best for the public library to create its own book lists for this age group.

To begin with, it can be helpful to obtain a copy of the school's summer reading list and annotate it according to what is available in your library's collection and where it can be found on the shelves. Though some school districts keep their reading lists on their websites, where they can be accessed by the public, it is a good practice to contact the schools before the summer even begins so that you have plenty of time to make notes on the list and to supplement your collection where needed. By going over the list carefully before patrons begin asking for the books, you can educate yourself about which books might be difficult to find, which are available at other locations within your library system, and which you simply cannot provide for patrons. This prevents you from being blindsided by many requests for the same book and allows you to provide the best customer service possible to families struggling with summer reading assignments.

Once you have made an effort toward assisting patrons with their school-assigned reading, it is time to shift gears toward the pleasure reading aspect of the summer reading program. While some kids may only focus on their school assignments all summer, many others will be looking to you for assistance in finding titles to read for fun. You can make at least some of these questions easier on yourself and other library staff by creating your own library-specific book lists.

There are five steps to creating a useful and appealing book list:

1. Brainstorm topics. The first step is always to brainstorm ideas for book list topics. During the summer, you will probably focus first on books that connect in some way with your summer reading theme. As you brainstorm around whichever topic is serving as your theme, think as broadly as you can. An ocean theme, for example, can include ocean animals, the beach, the water cycle, the globe, ships, and international travel. An exercise theme can include fiction and nonfiction about sports, games, the outdoors, healthy eating, air quality, and the human body. Once you have established a few topics connected with your theme, consider other areas of interest you are likely to be asked about. These may include read-alikes for a popular book of which you will have limited copies, books connected to a film that will be released during the summer, or titles by an author who might be visiting your community soon.

2. Make lists of titles. After the initial brainstorming, the next step is to begin listing titles that suit the topics you have selected, along with their call numbers. At the start of this process, simply list books as you think of them or as you discover them in the catalog. Make sure to include fiction and nonfiction titles, as well as books available in audio format, graphic novels, e-books, and anything else patrons might not easily find on their own by simply browsing. When you have good, lengthy lists for each topic, begin to pare them down according to whether books are missing or damaged, whether they are too popular to be expected to be on the shelves regularly, and whether each book is truly suited to the topic for which you originally thought of it. In general, a good book list will have fifteen to twenty titles.

3. Write annotations. Even though your book lists will be organized by topic, readers will still want to know something about each title to help them decide if they want to read it or not. You can help readers make their decisions by writing a sentence or two to accompany each title. These annotations should briefly tease what each book is about and indicate the genre to which it belongs. The reader can always rely upon the book jacket for a more complete description, but having your annotation on the book list helps them decide which books to pull from the shelves in the first place.

4. Make a note of reading levels. As mentioned earlier, reading levels are often important to parents, even if they feel overly restrictive to librarians. When you provide a book list, you should expect at least some parents to ask you for the reading levels associated with the listed books. You could look these up individually each time a patron approaches with a question, but it is a better practice to look them up ahead of time and keep them on hand for any parent or child who asks. To avoid child patrons pigeonholing themselves based on reading level, it is probably best not to print reading levels on the book lists that you make available

to the public. Still, it can be useful to create a version of each list that does list the levels so you can hand them to the patrons for whom they will be helpful. At the very least, in the spirit of good customer service, the library staff should be able to supply the reading level when asked.

5. Publish lists. When you are ready to make your book lists available to kids and their families, be sure to make them available in formats that patrons are likely to use. Print them out on regular printer paper and leave them on your desk or in another space where patrons typically come to pick up library-related literature. Create bookmarks listing the titles and annotations and hand them out to kids when they sign up for the program or attend library events. Publish the lists on the library's website with direct links to the holdings for each title and PDFs available for use on smartphones or to be printed at home.

Summer Reading Events for Ages Six to Twelve

The school-age events that your library hosts during the summer reading program can be as simple or as elaborate as you would prefer. This section provides some tried-and-true event ideas for ages six to twelve that can be adapted to suit most themes.

Hands-On Learning Opportunities

A wonderful component of any summer reading program is any event where kids have the opportunity to experience something new in a tactile way. These "hands-on" learning opportunities can be found in many different areas of interest, so it is easy to find the type of event that will connect best with your summer reading theme.

Any time the theme is connected to animals, habitats, nature, or being "wild about reading," a visit from a live animal is always welcome. Representatives from local zoos, animal hospitals, and rescue centers are often available to bring in animals for a visit. These visits may include opportunities for kids to hold, pet, or touch the animals. Even when the theme is not directly related to animals, you can easily connect this type of program to an overall interest in reading by reading a story about the animal at the event or inviting kids to read to the animal, as is often done with therapy dogs. Figure 4.1 shows a wildlife expert sharing a live snake with a group of children during a special summer reading event.

When science is the focus of the summer reading theme, hands-on experiments can be a great way to draw kids into the library. If the theme has a specific focus on electricity, you could present experiments involving batteries, static, and circuits. When the theme is focused on water, you could have the kids learn about sinking and floating, solubility and insolubility, and heating and cooling. Environmental science might inspire art projects using recyclable materials or planting projects where each child plants a seed to grow his or her own plant. Librarians can facilitate these events or they can invite local science experts, such as teachers, to the library to share their knowledge. Glaxo Smith-Kline also offers a Science in the Summer program in some states, in which accomplished scientists come to the library every day for a week to teach children about a specific scientific area. Information on this program is available at scienceinthesummer.com.

Other hands-on learning opportunities could include a book-making class (which, because it focuses on reading, is connected to any theme), a workshop in which kids learn

Figure 4.1. A wildlife expert shares a snake with a summer reading event audience. *U.S. Air Force photo by Rebecca Amber*

to create art in the style of a famous artist or illustrator (perfect for themes connected to creativity and the arts), and dance clinics where kids learn new dance movements from professionals in the field (which is the perfect accompaniment to music, movement, art, and dance themes).

Book Discussions

By offering book discussions for school-age kids in the summer months, libraries can help promote not just reading skills but the skills required to express one's thoughts and opinions about books. Book discussions are always timely during the summer reading program since they are all about reading. If you wish, you can also tailor your book discussion's focus to suit a specific theme.

One way to do this is to simply choose a book that matches the theme. This is an especially easy approach in years when the theme connects directly to a specific literary genre, such as mysteries or sports stories. Even without a clear connection to a genre, however, it is usually possible to find a good book that matches some aspect of a given year's theme.

Another relatively simple approach is to invite readers to come to your book discussion dressed as characters from the book they are reading. This type of book discussion works especially well with themes connected with clothing, hats, self-expression, drama, and imagination. For a food theme, put a spin on this idea and have your readers bring in characters' favorite foods instead.

Another possibility is to invite guests from your community to participate in your book clubs. If your summer reading theme is family, invite kids to bring a family member with them to book club meetings. If the theme centers on community helpers and heroes, seek out firefighters, police officers, or other emergency personnel who might be willing to talk with kids about the book they are reading and to provide real-life context for the story. Sports figures from local teams would also make great guests during years when the theme is related to sports, games, and play, as would local artists and authors when the theme is focused on the arts.

Beginning Reader Story Time

Your efforts to assist newly independent readers in their journey toward fluency are often more effective if you offer summer events specifically for this age group. A beginning reader story time is a great way to get to know the beginning readers who are participating in summer reading, and it is appealing to parents who are concerned about their kindergartners, first graders, and second graders maintaining the progress of the school year while school is not in session.

The format for a beginning reader story time can vary greatly depending on the librarian's personal style, the needs of the community, and the technology available in the space where the story time is held. Any of the following activities can be appropriate for use in this type of story time:

- Read-alouds, where the librarian reads and the attendees listen
- "Read-alongs," where the librarian and attendees take turns reading aloud or participate in choral readings together
- Literacy games, played either with physical game pieces or using a digital app
- Poems and rhymes, especially those that can be acted out or become interactive in some way
- "Write and draw" activities, where readers are asked to both write and illustrate a short piece related to the focus of the story time

The purpose of a beginning reader story time is not to teach children how to read. Rather, this story time seeks to support new readers in practicing skills they have already acquired and to keep those skills sharp between the end of one school year and the beginning of the next.

Reader's Theater

If you would prefer to break out of the traditional story time setting and try something even more interactive with your school-age summer readers, Reader's Theater can be a great way to do that. At a Reader's Theater event, participants read from scripts based on books, short stories, fairy tales, and other literary forms in order to practice reading aloud with expression. You can always write your own scripts, but they are also widely available from a variety of sources, including

- Aaron Shepard's website (www.aaronshep.com)
- Stories to Grow By (www.storiestogrowby.org)
- Dr. Chase Young (www.thebestclass.org/rtscripts.html)

- Busy Teachers Cafe (www.busyteacherscafe.com/literacy/readers_theater.html)
- Giggle Poetry (http://gigglepoetry.com/poetrytheater.aspx)
- Leveled Readers' Theater series by Evan Moor
- *Folk & Fairy Tale Plays for Beginning Readers: 14 Reader Theater Plays That Build Early Reading and Fluency Skills* by Immacula Rhodes (2010)
- *Readers Theater for Building Fluency: Strategies and Scripts for Making the Most of This Highly Effective, Motivating, and Research-Based Approach to Oral Reading* by Jo Worthy (2005)

When you host a Reader's Theater event, it is a good idea to ask participants to register ahead of time so that you know how many scripts to print out and how many roles you will need to have available to make sure everyone can participate. Another option is to avoid using scripts with many parts and to use shorter scripts instead so that you can assign more or fewer roles to each participant depending on attendance. Whichever approach you take, it is a good idea to assign the roles randomly by having kids choose from a hat or basket. This way you do not spend a lot of time working out who will play which part and you can spend as much of the event as possible actually reading and enjoying the scripts.

Art Contest

A perfect way to have fun with any summer reading theme is to challenge each summer's participants to an art contest. Tailor the focus of your contest to match the summer theme in some way. For a space theme, you might consider projects about rockets, planets, and the moon, whereas for a gardening theme, you might focus on trees, flowers, and insects. Whatever the theme, provide rules for your contest stating the age limit, due date of projects, and any other parameters you deem appropriate, including materials to be used and any size or safety restrictions you may have.

After the contest submissions have been collected, instead of worrying about who "wins" the contest, give each project a reward in its own unique category. These can include prizes for things like the most creative use of color, the most realistic-looking project, or the most imaginative idea. It is not necessary to brainstorm the award categories ahead of time; instead, it usually works best if you come up with a reward for each individual project after you have looked it over and spent some time with it. After each project has been given its prize, then create a display to show off participants' work.

Passive Events

If you have a hard time drawing in audiences for scheduled events, you can still provide activities for school-age kids by setting up passive events. A passive event is available whenever the library is open, and kids can participate in it with minimal involvement from library staff. Materials for the activity are left in a designated area along with instructions on how to participate and what to do when the activity has been completed (e.g., see a librarian to claim a reward, check off a box on a bingo card, etc.). Examples of passive events include

- Guessing games. These can take many forms. You can fill a jar with small items and ask kids to guess how many are inside. You can give clues as to the identity of a series of authors, characters, celebrities, or sports figures and have kids write down who they think the clues describe. Another option is to have a weekly trivia question or puzzle for kids to attempt to answer. Whichever approach you take, make sure there is a place for kids to turn in their answers and a way for them to find out the correct answer when the game ends.

- Scavenger hunts. A scavenger hunt can be a great passive event provided you can hide clues in places where they are not likely to be disturbed by regular library use. To put together a scavenger hunt, choose a theme and eight to ten locations in the library where clues can be hidden. Write a set of clues that will lead children on a clear path through the hunt. When you have a full set, hide them and test out the hunt yourself to make sure that all clues lead to the correct next location and that children will be able to reach the clues when they find them. If you are concerned about encouraging a lot of noisy foot traffic in the library, you can also provide a digital scavenger hunt that sends kids to different kid-friendly websites, databases, and library catalog entries. For this type of hunt, provide all clues ahead of time and assign a task to be completed at each site, such as looking up a fact or writing down a word or phrase. The hunt is finished when all tasks are complete.

- Printable word puzzles. Many school-age kids love word searches, crossword puzzles, codes, and other word puzzles. Create or find puzzles of this type online (or in your summer reading manual) and print them out to leave on tables in the children's area. Keep track of how many you print so that even if you do not see kids working on them, you will have an idea of how many were interested enough to take one. For more challenging puzzles, consider offering a prize (or credit toward a bingo card or checklist) for those who finish them.

- Open-ended art projects. Art projects requiring no particular skill that must be taught by an instructor are perfect activities to have available in the library all day. These can include completely open invitations to design one's own project using materials like pipe cleaners, buttons, ribbon, and other miscellaneous supplies, or they can be more structured projects, such as creating beaded jewelry, designing a collage of magazine clippings, or weaving friendship bracelets. Upon completion of their projects, encourage kids to take them home or provide a display area to showcase their creativity. Figure 4.2 shows a group of children painting flower pots in the library as part of a summer reading program.

Established Events

Finally, you should never discount the possibility of offering during the summer successful events your library has already implemented. If things like LEGO club, makerspaces, gaming, and STEAM (science, technology, engineering, arts, and mathematics) activities have been popular in your library, there is no reason to stop offering them during the summer just because they might not match the theme. The public is generally much less concerned with the summer reading theme than library staff are, and kids will attend events they like no matter how tightly or loosely connected to summer reading they might be.

In some situations, these staples of your events calendar might be an especially good match for the summer reading theme. For example, gaming events are strongly connected to themes related to play, games, and recreation, while STEAM and makerspace events can connect with themes related to the sciences, architecture, and the environment. When

Figure 4.2. School-age library patrons paint flower pots during summer reading. *Photo by Lance Corporal Ali Azimi*

you have a popular event that connects to the theme, certainly feel free to emphasize these connections in order to draw in new participants. In the reverse situation, where the theme does not seem connected in any way to your most popular events, use the popularity of these events to get kids interested in the summer reading program. Kids who are already in a regular habit of coming to the library for an event they especially love are often happy to join the summer reading program since they already have a favorable opinion of the library and its staff.

The bottom line is that you may not have to change anything to provide successful events for your summer reading participants. If your events schedule is not broken, there is no reason to fix it just for the sake of meshing your activities with the summer reading theme. It can be a reasonable decision to simply continue with some or all of your school-year events during the summer.

Serving Summer Camps

In many communities, especially in urban areas, summer reading programs attract not just families but also summer camps and other groups that make use of the library during the summer. It can be challenging to meet the needs of these groups, which often appear suddenly with many questions and demands, but it is worthwhile to foster relationships with these organizations, as they help libraries reach children who might not otherwise make contact and they fulfill many librarians' requirements to participate in outreach service.

To avoid a stressful and difficult experience working with summer camps, the best thing is to be proactive. Instead of waiting for camps to approach you, which they often

ABOUT SUMMER READING CLUBS

Some libraries have moved away from the concept of summer reading programs and instead invite kids to sign up for a summer reading club. These programs are run very similarly to the summer reading programs this book has described so far, but instead of offering individual events on various days throughout the summer, many of these libraries offer club meetings.

Summer reading club meetings occur weekly (or sometimes biweekly or monthly). At each meeting, members of the club (registered summer reading participants) report to library staff about their reading and then participate in an activity related to the summer reading program in some way. By having these club meetings, libraries make it easy for kids to check in with the library about their reading on a predictable schedule, and they make it easier to find an audience for each activity they wish to offer. Any of the events mentioned in this section can be suitable activities for a summer reading club. Indeed, some events will attract a greater audience at a club meeting than they would as stand-alone events.

do after the summer has already begun, reach out to representatives from these organizations well in advance. Find out from them whether the camp plans to use the library this summer, and if so, whether they will register the children in their care for the summer reading program. Also find out whether the camp will be making regular visits to the library and whether they will expect library staff to have an activity planned for them. Let the camps know what dates are available for their visits, and set a deadline by which each camp must let you know of their plans. By discussing scheduling with camp representatives ahead of time, you send the important message that, of course, the library is happy to host a camp visit and to have campers participate in summer reading but that the library cannot accommodate last-minute visitors who show up unannounced.

When coordinating with camps, also make sure the camp representatives understand the role of library staff when their campers are in the library. Explain the library's behavior policy and the fact that library staff can never act in loco parentis or discipline any of the camp's charges. Also make it very clear that camp staff is responsible for the campers and that they must remain in the library with the group during their visits. Especially in cases where camp counselors are young or inexperienced, they may simply not realize how supervision and behavior are handled in a public library setting. By explicitly stating this information, you eliminate any possibility of misunderstandings. You also want to make sure you do not allow a summer camp to run itself in the library. Some camps, especially those that meet in parks or do not have a designated indoor space, will try to use the library as a central meeting place. If this happens at your library, be sure to explain any policies your library has about running a business out of a library building and consult with supervisors and administrators as needed to help with the situation.

When setting up expectations, also be very clear about the types of activities you can offer for the camp. Camps sometimes come to the library with a list of things they want the librarian to do for their kids, many of which are simply impossible to accomplish while also maintaining regular library operations. Certainly, be willing to provide the basics of a library visit, including a tour, book talks, and the opportunity to borrow materials, but do not feel obligated to offer extra activities that would take significant time away from helping other summer reading participants. Whenever possible, try to invite camps to attend large-scale events such as musical performances or other scheduled events for which you might not otherwise have a large audience.

When it comes to registering campers for summer reading and tracking their progress, make sure to use a bulk registration method so that you do not spend a lot of extra time processing individual registration forms. Also make sure to provide camp counselors with a detailed set of instructions for what the children are expected to do in order to report their reading progress. Make it known to the counselors what the summer reading prizes are and what children must do to be eligible to win. Camp counselors who have not participated in summer reading since they were children themselves might have preconceptions about summer reading programs that can lead to misunderstandings if you are not up front about how your program runs.

Finally, be sure to keep detailed notes about your experiences with each camp that you serve during the summer. This information is helpful to look back on when planning future programs, but it is also invaluable for your successor to have should you ever leave your position. With your notes, be sure to include contact information for all the camps so you can use it to issue reminders during the year about when camps should get in touch about summer reading participation and so that you can pin down each camp's visiting schedule again when you plan for next year.

Key Points

This chapter has covered many of the key issues you must consider when providing summer reading programs for school-age kids.

- Make it easier for readers at different levels to compete by breaking the age range down into smaller groups, using time, a bingo card, or a checklist to track reading progress or having kids compete against themselves instead of each other.
- To be sure school-age kids will want to participate in summer reading, consider how your program handles recordkeeping, technology, reading levels, and design of promotional materials.
- Appropriate prizes for school-age kids include small giveaway items, special events to attend, participation in a communal display or art project, and recognition in a library newsletter or website article.
- In addition to book lists provided by the schools, which the library should review and annotate prior to the start of the summer reading program, librarians should also make their own book lists to suit the summer reading theme and other hot topics in which the community is interested.
- Successful school-age summer reading events include hands-on learning opportunities, book discussions, read-aloud events, art contests, passive events, and previously established and popular library events.
- To avoid misunderstandings, difficulties, and added stress, be proactive when providing outreach to camps and other organizations during the summer reading program.

In the next chapter, you will learn how to develop an appealing summer reading program for teens.

Summer Reading Programs for Teens

Why Include Teens?

PROVIDING A SUMMER READING PROGRAM FOR TEENS can have benefits for both the library and its teen patrons. There are four main reasons to offer a teen summer reading program:

1. To provide academic support. Just like younger students, teens can fall victim to summer learning loss if they do not read during the summer. Middle schools and high schools are even more likely than elementary schools to give summer reading assignments to their students. A reading program that offers incentives for its participants provides additional motivation and accountability for teen readers who may not necessarily continue to read all summer on their own.

2. To retain participants who have aged out of the school-age program. Children who are accustomed to participating in summer reading each year are likely to want to continue, even if only out of a sense of habit or tradition. By establishing a summer reading program for teens, you make it possible for patrons who are now too old for children's programs to continue participating in a way that feels comfortably

age appropriate. In many cases, children's program participants have been coming to the library during the summer for their whole lives; it would be a shame to see them break this habit because the library does not have a program for them.

3. To promote reading for pleasure. According to a 2013 study by the National Center for Education Statistics, only 28 percent of kids between ages twelve and fourteen and only 24 percent of kids between ages fifteen and seventeen read for fun five to seven days a week (Rideout, 2014). The study also showed that 33 percent of thirteen-year-olds read for pleasure two times a year or less. For seventeen-year-olds, the number is slightly higher (45 percent) but still less than half (Rideout, 2014). These statistics suggest an opportunity for teen summer reading programs to help kids in this age bracket rediscover (or perhaps discover for the first time) the joy of reading for fun. Because libraries are not beholden to specific curricula, standards, or goals, they are uniquely positioned to provide teens with a relaxed environment where they can discover books they will love without the pressures often placed on them by teachers and other influences.

4. To establish a teen patron base. Teens, especially those who are not yet old enough to work or drive, tend to be busier during the school year than they are in the summer. If you only offer teen programming during the school year, you may find that even those teens who are interested are unable to attend due to sports practices, after-school activities, and other commitments. In the summer, though, teens often have more free time, and they (and their parents) are looking for ways to spend that time constructively. Hosting a teen summer reading program allows you to discover who the teens are in your community and to help them realize all that the library can provide for them. Once they have had a positive summer experience, these teens may be more willing to work with you on establishing some year-round activities that suit their needs and schedules.

Encouraging Teens to Participate in Summer Reading

Teens visit libraries for many different reasons. It is likely that on any given summer day, the teens using your library are a mix of readers and nonreaders. Teen patrons who come to the library specifically to browse and borrow books most likely already have a strong motivation to read, and they may not need any encouragement at all to sign up for your program. For those who have not yet found that motivation, however, there are a variety of subtle things you can do to make your program appealing to them as well. These include developing a low-pressure program, making an example of yourself, showing off your readers' advisory skills, making the most of school visits, and promoting summer reading all year round. Each of these is explored in greater detail in this section.

Develop a Low-Pressure Program

When you develop your library's summer reading materials for teens, do your best to present your program as low pressure and relaxed. Teens who are out of the habit of reading may think of it as a cumbersome, time-consuming task. Instead of challenging them to read an intimidating-sounding number of books or pages throughout the whole summer, give them smaller, more manageable goals. Examples might be completing a variety of tasks with point values, filling in a bingo card that includes different genres and formats, or reading for a set period of time each day. These methods take the focus off a larger end goal and instead give the teens something concrete to work on each day. It might feel impossible to complete five novels in a summer but much simpler to read for fifteen minutes every day.

It also helps to avoid introducing too much competition into your teen summer reading program. While established readers will probably participate whether there is a competitive element or not, nonreaders can easily become intimidated by trying to keep up with those who go through many books very quickly. If you offer a prize for your teen program, it is best to select the winner according to a raffle where all readers who complete the program have an equal chance of winning or to reward each individual participant with a small token when each one completes the program. This will prevent teens who are not strong readers from assuming they will never win a prize and therefore choosing not to participate at all.

As much as possible, you also want to avoid taking an overly academic approach to your teen program. While you do want to make it known that assigned summer reading titles do count toward summer reading, you do not want to dwell so heavily on assigned reading that teens develop an unpleasant association with the library or begin to think of the summer reading program as a chore. Instead of focusing just on the academic side of things, make it clear in your summer reading materials that all types of reading count and that the library does not concern itself with reading levels.

Finally, since teens are so drawn to social media and mobile devices, a summer reading program might fit more easily into their lives if it also involves technology. Using a digital tracking method for summer reading progress and hosting challenges on popular social media platforms such as Instagram and Snapchat helps teens see the library as relevant to their daily activities and makes it easy for them to incorporate summer reading into their regular media use.

Make an Example of Yourself

Teens often develop friendly relationships with the staff members in charge of library teen departments, especially if those teens spend significant amounts of time in the library. Since your teen library users probably already know you and like you, they might be willing to follow your example. To make it known that you are also participating in summer reading, make it very easy for teens to discover your reading habits. There are several ways to do this:

- Keep a small display of young adult books you have recently read or are currently reading on the public desk while you are working. (Make sure these are additional copies of titles you are reading and not copies you have checked out!) Next to them place a sign reading something like "Miss Sarah's Current Summer Reads." This lets teens know that not only do you read, but you read teen books that might interest them. The display also makes a great conversation starter with both readers and nonreaders. Even a teen who makes a disparaging remark about a book you are reading is engaging with reading material on some level and providing you with a jumping-off point to recommend a book he or she might like better. You may need to adjust your reading habits slightly to ensure that this display covers a variety of formats and genres, but doing so can only help you know your collection even better.

- Post your own summer reading progress in a public place. One of the best ways to promote summer reading is to challenge yourself to complete the same program as the teens in your library. Hold yourself accountable to this task by posting your progress on a bulletin board or other display so teens can see that you are reading along with them. Teens tend to give more credibility to adults who do not just ask them to do things but who are willing to participate alongside them. By charting your summer reading progress publicly, you show that you are willing to put your money where your mouth is, and you might inspire teens with a competitive spirit to try and out-read you. (Adults are less intimidating competitors than fellow teens.)
- Get caught reading. Generally, it is considered bad form for a librarian to read while on duty, but with teens it can sometimes be worth setting aside other work for a few moments here and there so they can catch you in the act of reading. Teens who see you reading may be inclined to ask you about your reading material, or, especially if it is something of high interest, such as a popular manga title or a teen-interest magazine, they may have already read it and wish to discuss it with you. Once you have them discussing reading material with you, then you can let them know that reading of this type counts toward the summer reading program.
- Read books you know your teens are reading. If a certain book or series has become popular in your library, begin reading it and share your honest thoughts with teens who have read it. Even if they disagree with your point of view, a conversation with you helps them to see the fun that can come from discussing books outside of a classroom environment.

Show Off Your Readers' Advisory Skills

Teens love to challenge adults. Give them a fun reason to do so by inviting them to try to stump you on your knowledge of teen literature. Whenever teens seem reluctant about signing up for summer reading, let them know that you will guarantee that you will either find them a book (or other type of reading material) that will interest them or you will give them a small prize as a consolation for not being able to do so.

Undoubtedly, some teens will stump you with intentionally impossible requests, but this is not really a defeat. By the time you have admitted that you have been stumped, you have already shared multiple titles with the teens who challenged you, thereby enlightening them about what the library has to offer. Though the teens may not take home anything you recommended that day, they may return to the library with future requests and eventually land on a book they really do want to read. If the challenger is accompanied by friends, as is often the case, you may also find that others want to take the books you suggest, even if your challenger does not.

Make the Most of School Visits

Because of the way the school day is often scheduled in middle schools and high schools, it can sometimes be more difficult to have successful school visits in these buildings than in the elementary schools. Since a school visit is really only worth your while if it results in at least a few students participating in summer reading, it is important to make the most of these opportunities, however they present themselves. Regardless of whether you are asked to speak to classes of students, to a school-wide assembly, or just to individual kids who happen to pass by your table in the hallway, the key to a successful school visit for teens is to make it personal. Teens are very social creatures, and they will be most compelled to participate in an activity when it involves spending time with people they like. For teens to want to spend the summer visiting the library to participate in your program, they first need to feel a connection to you.

When you visit a school, make sure you appear friendly and approachable to all the teens you encounter. If you have the opportunity to meet with students individually or in small groups of friends, take the time to get to know them and begin building up trust. Instead of giving the same spiel every time a student approaches you, ask the teens questions about their own reading habits, use of the library, and summer plans. Talk to them in a friendly way about how the summer reading program fits with what they might already be doing, and let them know about aspects of the program you think they will like based on what they have said.

In larger groups, it can be more difficult to make a personal connection, but it helps if you can tell an entertaining story about yourself that makes you come across as approachable, interesting, and relatable. This might be an anecdote from a past summer reading experience in your library career or a library-related story from your own teen years. Also make sure to issue invitations to come visit you at the library. To motivate kids to follow through on these invitations, offer a trivia question or some such challenge and promise a small prize to any student who comes to the library with the correct answer.

However you are able to interact with students, it is beneficial to do so. Teens are more likely to participate in programs run by adults they like, and though you should never use your personal relationship with a student to manipulate her or him into participating in summer reading, the presence of an adult they enjoy being around can be a strong motivator for many teens.

Promote Summer Reading All Year Round

Probably the best thing you can do to get your teen audience excited about summer reading is to talk about it all year round. This way teens have lots of time to ask questions about the program and to provide you with their valuable input about when they are available to participate and what kinds of activities they might enjoy. Here are some suggestions for things you can do to build summer reading buzz well in advance of summer vacation:

- Events calendar. If you have an events calendar on your website, or in a printable format, list summer reading as an annual event and include the dates for the current year. To help build anticipation, you could also include a countdown to summer reading, listing how many days are left until the next program kicks off.
- School visits. Whenever you speak to school groups, either in the library or off-site, mention to them that a summer reading program happens every year and that you look forward to having them participate. Let them know where they can find out more information when the program gets closer and what is required for them to register.
- Theme reveal. If your library selects its own theme, or if your state's theme is not known to the teens in your community, host a theme reveal party where the teens find out together what the summer reading focus is for the year. Adding an air of mystery to your summer reading promotion is a great way to draw kids into the

program well before it begins and to seek feedback from teens about what they might like to see happen during the summer itself.

- Printable materials. Welcome packets for new teen library cardholders, bookmarks inside of new and favorite teen books, and even signs sharing testimonials from past summer reading participants are all subtle but effective ways to remind teens about summer reading all year long.

⊚ Prizes for Teens

As previous chapters have mentioned, there are compelling arguments on both sides of the question of whether summer reading programs should award prizes. Assuming you have chosen to reward your teen participants with either tangible or experiential prizes, this section provides suggestions of age-appropriate rewards in both categories.

Tangible Prizes for Teens

As long as the rewards suit their interests and maturity level, teens can be satisfied with a wide variety of tangible prizes, both large and small. Teens typically have a better understanding than their younger counterparts of the fact that they may not win a raffle. Therefore, you can usually raffle off big-ticket items for this age group without worrying about hurt feelings. Teens will be disappointed when they do not win, but in general they do not have their hearts set on beating the odds and being the one to take home a new bike, game system, e-reader, and so on. They have the maturity to understand the chances of winning and to lose gracefully.

Some teens are motivated by the possibility of winning a book at the end of the summer reading program. This is generally not a great way to reward teens who were reluctant about reading in the first place, but it can be the perfect way to acknowledge the hard work of teens who enjoy reading. If you do not have the funding in your budget to purchase a brand-new book for every teen, considering using advance reader copies you pick up at conferences as prizes. Teen readers love the opportunity to read new titles by their favorite authors before they are published.

Other tangible prizes that appeal to teens include

- Coupons for free or discounted food from local restaurants
- Candy bars
- Ear buds
- Phone chargers
- T-shirts
- Tote bags
- Flash drives
- Tickets to sporting events
- Museum passes

Experiential Prizes for Teens

Teens do not necessarily need a tangible souvenir to take home as a summer reading reward. Teen summer reading participants can be just as happy with an experiential prize. These experiences can be as simple or as complex as you prefer.

Some libraries keep things very simple and offer a pizza party or ice cream social for all teens who complete the summer reading program each year. Food-related gatherings are usually well attended by this age group, and if you have a long-standing donor who provides the food each year, this can be the ideal way to recognize teen summer reading participants without negatively impacting the library's budget.

Other libraries place the focus of experiential prizes on the library staff itself. Teen librarians and other staff members may promise to do things like shave their heads, dye their hair, sit in a dunk tank, or engage in some other unexpected or slightly uncomfortable behavior in order to motivate kids to read. You should never promise to do something like this without first being sure it is allowed by your library's policies, but provided there is no rule standing in your way, these over-the-top gestures can be a great way to get teens to push themselves to read just a little bit more than they already might.

Another great experiential prize is the opportunity to read away one's fines. Teens with expensive fines to pay are often unable to afford their cost. By allowing teens to receive credit toward their fines by reading for a certain amount of time, you encourage them to read more and you help them bring their accounts back into good standing so they can continue borrowing books and other materials.

⑨ Teens as Summer Reading Volunteers

Aside from having them participate in their own reading program, another great way to involve teens in summer reading is to use them as volunteers. Teen volunteers are helpful to the library because, at no financial cost, they can help alleviate some of the burdens summer reading tasks place on librarians. Teens can assist with setup and cleanup at summer reading events, perform simple clerical tasks such as filing registration forms, prepare craft projects for the school-age and early childhood summer reading programs, and perform other summer reading–related tasks. Depending on library policy, teen volunteers may also be able to help with some of the more basic day-to-day operations of the library—for example, shelving materials, stamping new items, discarding weeded materials, and creating displays. Having teens available to perform some of these simpler tasks allows library staff more freedom to focus on the work only they can accomplish.

Library volunteer programs are also appealing to teens. Volunteering at the library is a great way for teens to gain work experience before they are old enough to have a paying job. Teens who wish to work at your library in the future will be especially interested in volunteering in order to get a foot in the door. Many teens are also involved in religious, civic, and school programs that require them to perform a set number of volunteer hours. Library volunteer programs can help them fulfill this requirement. Teens who have participated in a summer reading program as children but feel awkward about participating now that they are older might also feel more comfortable (and more mature) in a volunteer role.

The remainder of this section covers everything you need to know to establish a successful teen volunteer program as part of your summer reading program.

Finding and Selecting Volunteers

Once you have decided to include a volunteering component in your teen summer reading program, the first thing you need to do is get the word out about the volunteer opportunities available at your library. To promote your volunteer program, write up a brief description of what you are looking for in a volunteer. Include information about age requirements, minimum time commitments, and the application process, and share it widely both in the library and throughout the community. Effective methods for promoting a volunteer program include signs posted in the library, blurbs on the library's website, an article in the library's newsletter, social media postings, and any other means you typically use to convey information to your patrons. (The approaches described in chapter 7, "Promoting Your Summer Reading Program," will also prove useful.) Additionally, consider reaching out to organizations that have heavy contact with teens who might be interested in performing volunteer work. These include the local schools, civic groups with heavy teen participation, religious institutions with educational and social programs for teens, homeschool support groups and co-ops, and scout troops.

As you begin to hear from teens expressing an interest in volunteering, you will need to begin a screening process to ensure that the teens you select will be a good fit for the library. Chances are you will not be able to take on every teen who expresses interest, so it is important to have a hiring process in place to help you choose who your summer volunteers will be. This process should be somewhat similar to what you might use to hire a paid staff member and should include a written application as well as a short interview. On the application and in the interview, ask questions to ascertain the following:

- Why the teen is interested in volunteering at the library
- The type of volunteer work in which the teen is most interested
- Any special skills the teen might be able to bring to the volunteer position
- Availability of the teen to volunteer during library hours in the summer months
- Whether a parent or guardian has granted permission for the teen to volunteer
- Whether the teen has a required number of hours he or she wishes to complete
- Whether the teen requires paperwork to be filled out to certify completion of hours

Collecting answers to these questions helps you to determine which teens are truly serious about committing to volunteering and which teens are available to provide assistance during the hours when the library can benefit the most from their extra pairs of hands. Obtaining parental permission and information about any required documentation ahead of time also eliminates the potential for misunderstandings and last-minute confusion.

Training Volunteers

Once you have selected your teen volunteers, it is important to give them at least some training to familiarize them with the library environment and the specific duties they will perform. There are several ways to organize the training. The first is to require a mandatory orientation day for every volunteer. All the teens you have selected would come to the library at the same time, and all would receive the same information. This approach works well if you are taking on a small number of volunteers or if all the volunteers you have chosen will have the same or similar duties.

Another approach is to divide the volunteers into groups based on the duties they will perform. Teens in a given group would attend a training session together, which would be customized to address their specific duties. This method works well when you have to train many volunteers, provided you have enough staff available to manage hosting multiple training sessions within a short time frame.

The final method is to train each volunteer individually. This works well if you only have one or two volunteers or if your volunteers have such different schedules that it would be impossible for them to attend training at the same time. Individual training sessions might also be necessary for any volunteers who must miss a group training session due to illness or other obligations.

Putting Teen Volunteers to Work

After your volunteers have been through the application and training processes, they should be ready to begin work. As your volunteers undertake their summer duties, follow these rules of thumb to ensure a smooth transition and a positive experience for teens and library staff alike:

- Introduce volunteers to all staff and make sure it is clear which duties teens are (and are not) meant to perform. If teens will be working outside of the teen department, under the jurisdiction of another staff member, make sure this arrangement has been well coordinated and everyone understands the teen volunteer's role. If there is a misunderstanding between you and another staff member about a teen volunteer's participation in a particular event or task, discuss it privately without involving the teen in an awkward situation.
- Keep tabs on attendance. Make sure your volunteers have a sign-in procedure and that this procedure is followed even when you may not be in the building. Periodically confirm that teens are indeed working during the times they are signed in. Follow up with any volunteers who do not show up for assigned hours or who habitually leave early or "disappear" during their working hours.
- Always have work available for volunteer shifts. Ideally, you will have scheduled your volunteers on days when you know you will need their help. Sometimes, though, you may find that your plans have fallen through or that the library is having an unusually slow day, and you may not have as much work as you thought you would. In these situations, do not waste the volunteer's time. Brainstorm a list of tasks ahead of time so that you always have a backup plan, and do your best not to scramble to find something for your volunteer to do while he or she is waiting.
- Engage with volunteers as they work. While it is wonderful to have volunteers available to alleviate some of the pressure on library staff during a notoriously busy time of year, the volunteer experience will not be very valuable if you simply work on your own tasks and never interact with your volunteer. Be sure to check in with volunteers as they work and praise them for work well done, make corrections where there is room for improvement, and invite them to ask any questions that may come up during their working time.

Thanking Summer Volunteers

Though teen volunteers are already compensated for their volunteer work with work experience and credit toward volunteerism requirements, it is good form for librarians to acknowledge them in a formal way as well. The best way to do this is with a reception at the end of the summer. Order pizza or another food your volunteers enjoy and invite them to enjoy a free lunch or dinner. Print up certificates for each volunteer and hand them out in a brief ceremony celebrating all their hard work. Use the rest of the time to talk with your volunteers about their experience. Solicit feedback about what they liked and disliked so you can make changes to the program for the next year. The reception is also a great opportunity to take care of any paperwork that may have fallen through the cracks or arisen at the last minute.

Libraries with a very small number of volunteers may also choose to thank their teens with a small gift. A personal gift related to a teen's reading interests or a gift card to a local bookstore are both perfect tokens of appreciation in these situations.

⑥ Events

Summer reading events can be a great way to engage teens with the library whether they are enthusiastic readers or not. This section provides brief descriptions of different programs you might offer for teens during the summer months, along with suggestions for connecting them with themes.

Make a Book Quilt

Sometimes there is a book connected to your summer reading theme that becomes really popular, or a book that sees a resurgence in popularity due to an upcoming film release or even a book from the school summer reading list that teens really begin to enjoy during the summer. A great way to harness teen enthusiasm regarding this type of book is to invite teens to make a quilt in celebration of it.

Online vendors such as Oriental Trading and Discount School Supply sell classroom quilt kits that can be used for this purpose, but you can just as easily adapt the activity to suit materials you already have on hand or that you can include in library supply orders. The project requires

- Squares of fabric or construction paper (minimum nine)
- A hole punch or pair of scissors for cutting holes into the corners of each square
- Ribbon or yarn for fastening the squares together
- Paint or markers
- Glue
- Decorations, including glitter glue, buttons, ribbon, and other embellishments

To create the quilt, each teen in attendance designs at least one square. The design should be connected to the book in some way. It can feature a character from the book, a favorite quotation, an alternate cover, or even a particular scene. When each participant's square is designed and all glue and paint have been allowed to dry, the squares are tied together at their corners using ribbon or yarn.

Once the quilt is completed, it can be displayed in the teen area, preferably near copies of the book on which it is based. At the end of the summer, if the quilt is no longer needed in the library, it can be disassembled and the pieces given back to their creators, or if they do not wish to have it, it can be raffled off to a summer reading participant or passed on to the local media specialist to be displayed in the school library.

Host a Talent Show

In years when the summer reading theme is connected in some way to performance, music, the arts, or self-expression, a talent show can be the perfect event to complement your summer reading program. Here are the steps for putting together a teen talent show:

- Find an appropriate performance space. Talent shows can be held in a variety of spaces, from meeting rooms to library lawns to high school auditoriums. The key is to secure a space ahead of time so that you know if there are limitations you must set on the number of performers, the size of the audience, the length of the program, the kinds of technology performers can use, and so on. You will not be able to hold a talent show without a performance space, so you should not proceed until you are certain that your selected space has been reserved for your preferred date and time.
- Announce the talent show at least a month in advance. This gives teens in your community enough notice to decide which talent they will perform and time to practice and feel comfortable performing. When you ask for talent acts to participate, be sure to give them a deadline by which they must sign up in order to be included. If you will not be able to take everyone who signs up, determine a number that you will take ahead of time and accept that number of acts on a first come, first served basis.
- Preview all talent acts. Since the talent show is a public performance put on by the library, you want to be aware of its content prior to the day of the event. While it is not necessary to disqualify acts based on their quality, you do want to ensure that all performances will be in compliance with library policy and will be appropriate for the audience you will invite to attend. (Your standards will be different for a teens-only audience than for an audience that includes families and young children.) The easiest way to preview each talent is to set up a block of time on a particular day and have each teen come in to do a brief run-through of his or her proposed performance.
- Assign teens to run the show. While some teens love the spotlight, others would prefer to help out behind the scenes. When you advertise in the community looking for talent show performers, also seek out those teens who might be interested in creating programs, announcing the acts, acting as ushers, and filling any other roles that will make the talent show a success. Giving teens as much involvement in the event as you can helps them feel that the production truly belongs to them. This sense of ownership can easily lead to future teen-led library programs.

Some teens who have participated in talent shows in the past might expect there to be a competitive component to your show. If you do choose to have your performers compete against one another, be sure to select a panel of unbiased judges to determine the winners. Consider inviting at least one teen to judge, as well as other impartial community members, including teachers, library board members, and local government officials who do not know the teen competitors well.

If your talent show is not competitive, make sure teens know this ahead of time and find a way to acknowledge each teen's participation with a certificate, trophy, or other keepsake that can be saved as a souvenir of the experience.

Candy Bingo

Though it is a simple game, teens love to play bingo. In this variation, the players use candy (M&M's, Skittles, Hershey's Kisses, and so on) as bingo markers. At the end of the game, they eat the markers they have used.

The bingo cards themselves can be designed to match any theme. Online bingo card generators make it possible for you to make your own bingo cards using words or images of your own choosing. Even if your library does not use a theme, you can still create cards to go along with a particular book, series, movie, or other popular topic. Teens can play for fun, or you can award candy bars or bookmarks to the winners of each game.

Instagram Photo Challenge

Instagram is home to many photo challenges on many topics. These challenges typically occur over the course of a month, and participants are asked to take a photograph to fulfill a different prompt on each day of the month. This challenge format is ideal for engaging teens who are heavy social media users.

To put together an Instagram challenge for your summer reading program, first brainstorm a list of prompts. If you use a summer reading theme, try to connect your prompts to the theme. If your theme is too specific or if you do not use a theme at all, prompts related to reading or library use also work well. If you choose to follow the monthly format, assign each prompt to a date of the month when you will run the challenge. Otherwise, simply list the prompts the teens will need to complete in order to finish the challenge.

Once you have your list of prompts, create a simple graphic. This graphic should be a square of at least 1,080 pixels by 1,080 pixels that lists your prompts, provides a unique hashtag for the challenge, and identifies the name of your library and the title of your challenge. Upload this graphic to your library's Instagram account. (Details about registering for and using Instagram are covered in chapter 7, "Promoting Your Summer Reading Program.")

As teens upload their own photos, you will be able to see them by searching for or clicking on your selected hashtag. You can then comment on the teens' photos and share them on the library's other social media pages, as well as on the library's own website. Though many teens will find completing the challenge satisfying enough, you could also provide a prize or credit toward a large prize for those who participate and fulfill every prompt.

Book-Trailer Screening

Since all summer reading themes always involve reading itself, a book-trailer screening can be a part of your teen summer reading program each year. This is a great way to help teens find out about new books in a way that engages their interest in media. This is also a great way to promote books connected to your summer reading theme that might not be as popular as other titles frequently borrowed by your teen patrons.

To host a book-trailer screening, you need a room with audiovisual equipment, a selection of book trailers promoting books that your library owns, copies of the books advertised in the trailers, and, if your teens prefer, popcorn. Play book trailers for about twenty to thirty minutes while the teens watch and snack on popcorn. Then invite your teens to borrow the books that caught their attention. Because this program is relatively easy to put together, it might be possible to host one of these screenings as often as once a week if they are popular. For a twist, consider asking teens to create their own trailers to be screened at future sessions.

⌾ Key Points

This chapter has covered a variety of ways to ensure a successful summer reading program for teens.

- A summer reading program for teens provides academic support, helps retain summer reading participants who have aged out of the children's programs, promotes reading for pleasure, and establishes a teen patron base.
- To encourage teens to participate in summer reading, develop a low-pressure program, make an example of yourself, use your readers' advisory skills, make the most of school visits, and promote summer reading all year round.
- Appealing teen prizes include tangible rewards like books, flash drives, and T-shirts, as well as experiential rewards such as ice cream socials, librarians shaving their heads, and opportunities to read away fines.
- When taking on teen volunteers, have a screening process in place. Be sure to train volunteers, engage with them during their volunteer time, and thank them at the end of the summer.
- Simple and interesting summer reading events include making a book quilt, hosting a talent show, playing candy bingo, creating an Instagram photo challenge, and screening book trailers.

This concludes this book's section on summer reading programs for youth. Chapter 6 will focus on the development of summer reading programs for adults.

⌾ References

Rideout, Victoria. 2014. *Children, Teens, and Reading: A Common Sense Media Research Brief*. Common Sense Media, May 12. www.commonsensemedia.org/research/children-teens-and-reading.

Summer Reading Programs for Adults

⊚ Why Include Adults?

HOSTING SUMMER READING PROGRAMS FOR ADULTS is a relatively new phenomenon, and many communities have not yet caught onto the trend. While it may sometimes be difficult to accommodate yet another program during a time of year when the library is already in such high demand, there are several good reasons why libraries ought to consider putting an adult summer reading program in place:

1. To fulfill the library's mission statement. Libraries commonly include in their mission statements a goal of promoting a lifelong love of reading. Offering a summer reading program for adults demonstrates your commitment to this goal and helps you work toward achieving it. Adult summer reading programs also help libraries keep their teen audiences interested as they graduate from high school and move on to college and careers.

2. To allow families to participate together. Over the past decade, there has been a growing emphasis on the role of the parent in the development of children's literacy skills. Children learn to love reading when they see their parents enjoying it

themselves. By offering a program for adults, you affirm their role as models for their children and you encourage their own pleasure reading at the same time.

3. To meet more of your adult patrons. Adult patrons who like to read can be very elusive. Often they come to the library prepared with a list of the books they need, find them without librarian assistance, and then check them out using a self-service checkout machine. Because they are savvy library users, you may never have the chance to meet them unless you offer a program that encourages them to make contact. Summer reading programs typically require patrons to check in with a staff member at least once or twice throughout the summer in order to register, report progress, pick up prizes, and/or attend events. Providing these programs can be a great way to engage the reading public and really get to know these important members of your library community.

4. To build community. Though your adult summer reading program participants share a common love of reading, they may not know each other. Using your summer reading program as a means of building a network of these adult readers helps to strengthen the sense of community surrounding your library. This can be accomplished by hosting book clubs and other events that will bring together like-minded library users.

5. To promote your adult collections. Summer reading programs bring about great opportunities to create book lists, give book talks, and display hidden gems of your collection in order to encourage patrons to check out titles they might not discover on their own. If you have an overall goal of increasing circulation of adult materials, the summer reading program is a great way to encourage adults to borrow more.

Attracting Participants

Just as parents sometimes have to be convinced that summer reading is a good fit for their families, adult patrons may also need some encouragement before they agree to sign up for your summer reading program, especially if the program is new. There are several things you can do to make your program more appealing for the adults in your community. These include developing a well-thought-out program, reaching out to library users, and partnering with community organizations.

Developing a Well-Thought-Out Program

Because libraries are so accustomed to focusing on summer reading programs for children, an adult summer reading program can sometimes become an afterthought that is tacked onto the summer events calendar at the last moment. Programs that are thrown together haphazardly just before they begin are rarely successful, and they often create unforeseen extra work for staff and unnecessary stress for everyone involved, including patrons. Poorly designed programs can be confusing and cumbersome, and they can easily cause patrons to stop using your library or at the very least to avoid it during the summer months.

If you truly want to offer a viable program for adults, you will need to give it the same consideration and effort that you give to summer reading programs for other age brackets. This means creating an adult program unto itself, rather than just modeling the program after what is offered for children, and focusing on the needs and interests of your specific community. To ensure that your program is truly suited to your adult patrons, it can be helpful to create a separate set of goals for your adult summer reading program. These goals help develop your overall vision for the program and highlight the differences between the adult and youth programs at your library. Here are some potential goals you might strive to reach with your adult summer reading program:

- To see a certain number of adults complete the program
- To promote less popular areas of your adult collection
- To broaden individual patrons' reading horizons
- To encourage patrons to make more time to read
- To establish a long-term book club
- To increase attendance at adult programs
- To encourage a particular segment of the adult population (e.g., senior citizens, college students, etc.) to become more strongly connected to the library
- To highlight the different forms and formats reading material can take (graphic novels, audiobooks, e-books, etc.)
- To encourage discussion of books in your community

By explicitly stating what you would like to see happen in your adult summer reading program, you give yourself a clear path to follow as the program unfolds.

Reaching Out to Library Users

Though some adult patrons are always eager to participate in new library programs, many others will wait to be invited before they join in. As you begin to promote your adult summer reading program, take note of the patrons you interact with on a regular basis who might be interested in taking part. As you assist them at the information desk or check out materials to them, issue a casual, personal invitation to sign up for summer reading. A personal invitation from a librarian sends the message to patrons that the program truly is for them and that their participation is something you would value and appreciate. Sometimes a casual conversation about the program also helps disabuse patrons of any misconceptions they may have about the program and helps them realize that they would enjoy participating, even if they had not previously considered it.

Patrons who regularly attend library events or who are active members of the Friends of the Library are also likely to be interested in your summer reading program. Even before you begin formally planning and promoting summer reading, you can build some buzz for your adult program by letting your loyal event attendees know that it will be coming soon. These library "regulars" can help you spread the word, and they also provide a core group of participants on which to build a successful program.

Also make sure to reach out to regular library users who may not interact with you directly very often but who are enthusiastic readers. These include individuals who place holds on books from other libraries, borrowers of e-books and other downloadable materials, and patrons who rely solely on self-service checkout machines to borrow materials. To reach these patrons, slip flyers into books on hold and display summer reading information near the hold shelf and self-checkout machines. Also place ads and links for your summer reading program on any page of the library's website a user must pass through to access downloadable materials.

You are also likely to find enthusiastic readers among the parents of the children and teens participating in your youth summer reading programs. To invite parents to sign up for your adult summer reading program, include a blurb about summer reading on flyers for the children's and teen programs, especially those that are delivered to schools and sent home with students. When representatives from your library visit schools to promote summer reading, encourage them to tell students that the adults in their lives can be a part of the experience as well. Also be sure to announce adult summer reading activities at all story times and other programs where parents and caregivers are in attendance. Cross-promoting summer events for the different age groups allows you to reach adult patrons who might typically only visit the children's department.

Partnering with Community Organizations

In addition to working to attract regular library visitors and borrowers to your summer reading program, it is also beneficial to think outside the box and reach out to groups in your community who might be infrequent library users or even nonusers. Though it is possible to extend this kind of outreach on an individual basis, you can often cover a lot more ground if you partner with local organizations. These organizations already have active clients and members, so you can reach many individuals at one time, and you can delegate some of the promotional work to community leaders instead of library staff.

Some organizations to consider are

- Nursing homes and adult group homes
- Senior centers and recreation centers
- Local chapters of mothers' groups, such as MOPS and MOMS Club International
- Teachers' organizations
- Civic organizations, such as the Lions Club, Kiwanis, or Rotary
- Religious groups, especially those with established book clubs or lending libraries of their own
- Local government agencies (employees and clients)
- College and university campuses (faculty and students)

Reaching out to members of your community who do not regularly use the library not only helps to grow your summer reading program but also opens up opportunities for further partnerships and greater library use in the future.

Reading Goals and Reporting Methods

The reading requirements for your adult summer reading program should be easy to understand but difficult to complete in just a few days. Though your library's programs for children and teens might have a variety of tracking methods, involving recording minutes and pages read as well as titles, it is generally not necessary to ask adults to keep such careful records. Most adults who like to read do so regularly, and they are not necessarily in the habit of keeping track of anything other than the titles of books they have read. Asking patrons with established reading habits to add tedious recordkeeping to their schedules can cause them to burn out on your program quickly rather than encouraging them to meet the end goal. It is best to simply ask adults to keep track of the books they read.

When you ask adults to report their reading to the library, the best reporting methods are reading logs, bingo cards, and checklists, all of which are described in chapter 2, "Developing a Summer Reading Program." Which one you choose will depend on the goals you have established for your adult summer reading program and the interests and habits of your community. If your goals are simply to increase reading time among your patrons and to encourage them to provide feedback about books, a simple reading log will suffice. If you want to challenge your patrons to read more broadly, then a checklist or bingo card listing the categories from which they should select their books is more appropriate.

Whichever method you use, make sure that the challenge is not so narrow that it stifles readers' enjoyment of the books they borrow. Patrons should feel that they have the freedom to read what they like, and there should be no hidden personal or political agenda in the book categories you choose to include. Try to keep your categories general (romance rather than paranormal romance, biography rather than presidential biography, etc.) and allow patrons to interpret them broadly according to their own interests and point of view.

If you feel that asking adults to track their reading progress is not necessarily a good fit for your library, an alternative is to solicit book reviews from your summer reading participants. These reviews can be displayed in the library, published in the library's newsletter or website, or even compiled and printed to be given to all adult summer reading participants at the conclusion of the program. Patron book reviews are a great way to help promote both your summer reading program and your library's collection.

Rewards for Adult Summer Reading Participants

Unlike younger patrons, who might be motivated to read during the summer by the allure of a reward, adults who choose to sign up for summer reading rarely need the same encouragement. Adult summer reading participants already read for pleasure, so for them the appeal of the program is the chance to challenge themselves to read more, to interact with other readers during library events, and to simply celebrate reading as a hobby. If there is no additional funding in your budget to provide prizes for your adult summer reading program, this does not need to prevent you from moving forward with developing the program anyway. Prizes are by no means a necessary component of an adult summer reading program.

That said, many libraries do reward their adult summer reading participants for their achievements, and this is a perfectly valid practice. In some cases, these prizes are small, inexpensive giveaway items, such as bookmarks, printed book lists, pens printed with the library's logo, refrigerator magnets, paper fans, mouse pads, or bumper stickers. Other prizes might be more substantial, such as free books, tickets to local events, coupons for free food or merchandise from local businesses, or gift cards to bookstores. There are also libraries that offer a raffle at the end of the summer where selected summer reading participants win gift baskets, e-readers, lunch with authors, and other costlier prizes as the library is able to afford or receive as donations.

Another way to reward patrons who participate in your summer reading program is to host a reception at the end of the summer. This celebration can be something as simple as a coffee hour with light refreshments where participants can meet to enjoy the company of other readers and to recommend books to one another. If many of your adult summer reading participants are parents, it is also a nice gesture to recognize them along with their children at any end-of-summer party you have for your youth programs.

⌾ Scheduling Summer Events

Hosting adult events at the library during the summer is a great way to increase interest in summer reading participation and to give summer reading participants a reason to visit the library beyond just picking up materials and reporting reading progress. Though it is possible to have a successful adult summer reading program without hosting any specific summer reading events, it is usually desirable for libraries to host at least one or two special events during the program.

As you schedule and plan events for your adult patrons, there are several factors you will need to address. One is the varied makeup of your adult patron base. *Adults* is a broad term, and different segments within that population have different relationships to the library. Retired patrons, for example, can easily visit the library during the day and attend events in the mornings and afternoons. College students and young professionals, by contrast, are typically in class or at work during the weekdays and may only use the public library sporadically on nights or weekends. Patrons who rely upon public transportation to visit the library may only be available to visit during certain windows of time when buses, trains, and taxis are available, while parents may only visit the library during children's events or in the late afternoon between day camp dismissal time and the dinner hour. To help you figure out which programs to offer when, it is important to pay attention to the patterns of when patrons are most likely to stop by the library and to plan events for each patron group during the time when they are most likely to be able to attend.

Another important factor that can impact the planning of events for adult summer reading is the schedule for the children's and teen summer reading programs at your library. Especially if this is your first year offering an adult summer reading program, you may find yourself in stiff competition with the children's department for the use of meeting rooms, audiovisual equipment, and staffing for your events. To prevent a frustrating situation where adult programs are simply given whatever is left after the children's program has established its schedule, the events schedule for all departments should be created collaboratively very early on in the summer reading planning process. Though children's programs frequently meet during the daytime hours, this should not be used as a reason to automatically relegate all adult programming to the evening. Rather, it should be possible for every department to offer events at the times best suited to their intended audiences, even if it means some activities do not make it into the schedule.

Another scheduling consideration is the flexibility of your work schedule. Sometimes in order to offer events and activities at the most suitable time, it can be desirable for a librarian to work additional hours or to switch shifts in order to be present for a particular event. There may also be situations where you want to offer a morning program on a day when the library opens after noon or an evening program after the library has closed for business for the day. Though some libraries may have strict policies prohibiting staff from changing their schedules or from being in library buildings outside of regular hours, it can be worth exploring the possibilities to make it easier to offer events that will attract larger numbers of participants than you can bring in during regular business hours.

⑥ Event Ideas

There are many types of wonderful events you can offer during the summer. This section will explore some of the tried-and-true events that can bolster summer reading participation without creating a lot of burdensome extra work for library staff. The events discussed here fall into five categories: reading, community, technology, arts, and education.

Reading-Related Events

The most logical type of activity to accompany your summer reading program is an event centered on a love of books and reading. These events can be beneficial in two ways. They are appealing to those patrons who are already registered for summer reading, which helps you secure an audience and prevents a situation where no one shows up to a scheduled event. They also help you bring readers into the library, where you can provide them with information about the summer reading program. In many cases, libraries already have programs of this nature in place, so it is just a matter of scheduling them to suit the rhythm of summer in your community and tweaking them to suit a theme, if you are using one. The following are suggested reading-related events for your adult summer reading program.

Literature-Based Film Festival

Film screenings tend to be popular library events, and they are easy to put together. To organize a film festival with a strong literacy connection, first select a theme that relates closely to books. For instance, you might show a series of movies based on novels, a set of biographical films about well-known authors, or even multiple film adaptations of the same fairy tale or folktale for purposes of comparison. As you brainstorm possible films to include, confirm that your library has the proper license to show them to a public audience and that a playable copy of the film is available to you. Give your film festival a title that incorporates the theme that connects your chosen films, and promote the date and time for each screening.

To help promote your collection, at each film screening, display books and other library materials that connect with the theme or with an individual film and encourage attendees to borrow them. To promote community among participants, lead a group discussion following each film. Provide some background information about the way the film was adapted, the filming process, or anything else you can research, and prompt viewers to discuss the elements of the film that worked for them, as well as those that did not.

Unique Book Clubs

Many libraries already have established book clubs and, of course, members of those clubs will be welcome participants in your summer reading program. To add a spark to your summer reading program, however, it might be worth offering a new book club with a different creative concept. Here are some suggestions:

- Book pairings. Participants read related books in two different formats (picture book and novel, graphic novel and biography, poetry collection and travel book, etc.).
- "Book and Cook." Patrons read a book containing recipes and prepare the dishes to share as a group. The dishes can be prepared by participants offsite and brought

to the library, or if your library has a kitchen, cooking the dishes can be part of the book club meeting.

- Drama book club. Participants read a play or other script aloud together. (This concept also works with graphic novels, especially if images from the books can be displayed on a screen during the dramatic reading.)
- Family book club. Invite families to read classic family favorites together and come to the library to discuss them with other families. (Variations on this concept include mother/daughter and father/son book clubs and grandparent book clubs.)
- "Read Anything" book club. Participants read a book of their own choosing and then deliver a review to the club to encourage others to read it.

Book Talks

Voracious readers are always eager to hear about new titles, but they may not have a chance to chat regularly with a librarian. A book talk event, where a librarian introduces compelling reads from the library's collection, is a great way to satisfy your patrons' desires for new reading material and to increase circulation of certain titles.

To host a book talk, choose a diverse selection of titles from your adult collection (eight to ten books is a good target range). Acquire as many copies of the book as you can by placing holds from other library branches, and prepare a short teaser to generate excitement about each one. At the event, make copies of each book available so that readers who are drawn in by your book talks can borrow the ones that pique their interest. For a variation on this event, screen book trailers and/or videos of authors teasing their own books. Many of these are available on YouTube or through publishers' and authors' websites.

Blind Date with a Book

Another way for patrons who are enthusiastic about reading to discover new titles is through a Blind Date with a Book event. Many libraries offer this passive program to coincide with Valentine's Day, but it can work just as well during summer reading, especially because it is an ongoing event that can be incorporated into the daily operations of the library.

To get started, select a variety of books from your collection that might be a bit neglected or that have wide appeal to a general audience. Wrap these books in paper so that their titles are not discernible to patrons. Display the wrapped books in a prominent place accompanied by a Blind Date with a Book sign inviting patrons to take a chance on borrowing a book without knowing which title is it ahead of time. You can leave the wrapped packages completely unmarked or label them with a few clues as to their contents, such as genre, the length of the book, or the Dewey Decimal call number range from which it was taken.

Inside each book, include a comment card for patrons to share their reactions to selecting an unknown title. Provide a basket, box, or similar receptacle for patrons to return the cards upon completing their books. Periodically collect and display patron reactions on a testimonial bulletin board to help promote the event to other potential participants.

Literacy Workshops for Parents

If many of your adult summer reading participants happen to be parents, consider partnering with your library's children's department staff to provide a workshop on the role of parents in a child's journey toward learning to read. The workshop may include tips for reading aloud, an explanation of how children acquire early literacy skills, the opportunity to make story time props (such as puppets or flannel boards) to use at home, and even a tour of the children's department to help parents become better acquainted with how it is organized and laid out. If your library has enough staff available, you might even be able to offer the workshop simultaneously with a program for children so that parents have the opportunity to meet with other parents while their children are occupied by an activity.

Community Events

Summer can be a wonderful time of year for your library to connect more fully to its surrounding community. This can be accomplished in two ways: by partnering with community organizations to put on events outside of the library building and by inviting representatives from community groups into the library to be part of your events. This section provides a few examples of community events in which you can participate both in and outside of the library.

Offsite Outreach Events

Though many community members who are interested in reading already visit your library on a regular basis, there are still likely to be some residents who do not often come to the physical library building. If you find that it is difficult to attract participants to your in-house library events, you might have more success holding those same events at locations throughout your community. Bars and restaurants can make excellent venues for book clubs, while local bookstores and community centers might be able to help you bring in an audience for an author talk. Nursing homes and other residential facilities might enjoy having librarians visit to lend books and provide book talks, as well as to allow residents to participate in summer reading from the comfort of their own rooms. Though you may need to make some alterations to the events you would typically offer to make them suit an outreach environment, it is usually worth the effort to make those accommodations in order to connect with more of your community.

Community Poetry Reading

If you have access to a sizable indoor or outdoor performance space either in the library or in a facility belonging to another local organization, consider hosting a community poetry reading. Invite well-known members of your community—the mayor or town supervisor, the fire chief, the chief of police, the school superintendent, the bank president, your library director, and so on—to select their favorite poems to perform for a public audience. Arrange the performances in a pleasing order to create a program that highlights the library's relationship to others in the community and also inspires community interest in poetry. Be sure to have poetry collections available to check out, especially those that include the poems presented during the reading.

Local History Tours

Another interesting way to engage adult patrons, especially those with long-standing roots in your area, is to provide tours of interesting historic sites in your community (or a single walking tour of multiple sites, if geography permits). If the library houses information about these sites, delve into it as you prepare commentary to be given during the tours and make it known to your audience that they can follow up at the library for more information. If the information is housed instead by the historical society, consider partnering with that organization or inviting a representative from the society to conduct the tours on the library's behalf. If your library's building and/or grounds has historic significance, do not forget to include these in your tour as well. Local history events are great additions to summer reading programs with themes focused on architecture, community, and history.

Technology-Related Events

A very practical way to engage adult patrons during the summer months is to offer classes and workshops to help them become more familiar with different types of technology. This is a great way to highlight the many digital resources available through your library and to cut down on the frustration patrons experience when they do not quite understand how to use what is available. Technology-related events connect especially well with summer reading themes relating to communication, computers, and science. Several different workshop ideas are described in greater detail in this section.

Computer Classes for Beginners

Patrons who are not yet computer savvy can greatly benefit from a class that covers the basic skills librarians sometimes take for granted, including using email, searching the web, evaluating online information, and understanding social media. Ideally, these classes will be held in a computer lab or computer area with enough stations to allow each participant to have his or her own machine, but even if this type of space is not available, you can still teach the information in a lecture-style format and allow individuals to practice what they have learned on actual computers in one-on-one sessions or in small groups.

Summer can be a nice time to offer a class of this nature because there is not as much competition for computers from students as there is during the academic year and there is less chance of inclement winter weather preventing participants, many of whom are likely to be senior citizens, from showing up. Offering computer classes in the summer is also a great way to help students who are expecting to begin a new semester of college in the fall and parents who anticipate having to use online programs to assist children with homework assignments and to communicate with the local schools.

Device Clinic

Library patrons often come to information desks for assistance using various mobile devices and computers. It is not always possible to assist a patron in depth during a busy shift on the reference desk, but a scheduled clinic gives librarians the freedom to spend a bit more time troubleshooting a patron's particular issue. Depending on demand, you may choose to have a walk-in device clinic at certain predictable times that appear on the calendar each month or you may wish to have patrons make an appointment when their needs arise.

As you prepare to offer a device clinic, do your best to guess ahead of time what the commonly asked questions will be and prepare your approaches for handling them. Also consider creating printable handouts to send home with patrons after you have assisted them with these common issues, so they can refer back to everything you discussed when they have left the library. If it is difficult to staff a device clinic regularly, enlist the help of tech-savvy volunteers in your community who might be willing to pitch in and provide clinic service.

Another aspect of your clinic might be a digital device petting zoo. In a "petting zoo," you would allow patrons access to library-owned devices such as iPads, laptops, smartphones, e-readers, and gaming systems so they can test them out and evaluate what they might want to purchase or so that those who cannot afford to purchase at this time can still keep up with technology by learning how to use the newest available models.

Digital Downloads Workshop

Even tech-savvy library users can sometimes encounter difficulties navigating the different portals libraries use to provide access to e-books and digital audiobooks. Holding an introductory class that highlights the e-book providers used by your library and the nuanced differences between them is a great way to decrease patron frustration and to increase circulation of digital material. In situations where some books are only available digitally at your particular library, a workshop of this type also broadens the borrowing pool for patrons seeking to meet specific challenge goals associated with your summer reading program.

Invite patrons to bring their digital devices with them to the workshop so they can work through each step of the download process in real time with the device they will use to access materials at home. It is also helpful if the library has access to the same devices so that you can complete each step and ask patrons to follow your lead. After the workshop, provide patrons with printed instructions (or a webpage) to which they can refer the next time they try to download materials and you are not available.

Gaming

A fun way to engage adults through technology is to offer gaming events specifically for adults. These can include video game tournaments, *Minecraft* tutorials, coding workshops, and so on. An alternative to a technology-based gaming event might be an "unplugged" game night where you discourage the use of devices and provide traditional board and card games for patrons to play instead. An extension of this type of event might be an ongoing and recurring event, such as a chess club. Depending on the summer reading theme, you could also narrow the focus of your gaming events to games that are directly related to the theme you are using—for example, games from different countries for an "around the world" theme or games with a creativity component for a theme related to arts and imagination. Gaming itself also ties in with themes related to play, technology, and competition.

Arts Events

Arts events are perennially popular in public libraries, and this is as true in the summer as it is at any other time of year. If your library does not already offer opportunities for patrons to engage with the arts during the summer, or if you have had some success and would like to build upon it, consider adding one of these types of events to your summer calendar:

- Musical performances. Local musicians, as well as nationally recognized library performers, can be great additions to a library's summer events calendar. Use your library's own budget and space to host a concert, or consider partnering with other community organizations to put on a concert series. If you have a suitable space available, outdoor concerts do especially well in the summer months. Wherever the performance takes place, be sure to bring printed material that promotes the library and describes the summer reading program to distribute to potential new library users.
- Dance lessons. In addition to musical performances, demonstrations by dance groups also tend to be popular library events. These events can consist simply of performances, or they can include a practical element, where participants watch a demonstration and then receive an introductory dance lesson.
- Art classes. Seek out a local artist or art teacher to provide a simple art workshop for beginners at your library. At the conclusion of the class or series of classes, display participants' artwork in the library and host a reception to celebrate their accomplishments.
- Knitting circle. Knitting is a popular activity among adults of all ages. Encourage local knitting enthusiasts to visit the library by providing a space for them to knit and visit with one another on a regular basis throughout the summer. If you have veteran knitters with a desire to teach, you can also reach out to beginners and offer a class.
- Writers' group. Reading and writing are hobbies that go hand in hand for many people. To encourage aspiring writers, offer an opportunity for them to meet in the library and discuss their works in progress. If you have a relationship with any local authors, consider asking some of them to be guest speakers for the group or to run a workshop about a particular aspect of the writing process.

In years when the summer reading theme connects to a specific area of the arts, such as music, painting, or dance, it helps to schedule events centered on that particular focus. In other years, you may decide to host arts events where the artistic works themselves are all focused on the specific theme you are working with. For example, if the theme is animals, you might offer an art workshop focused on painting a portrait of the family pet. If the theme is technology, you could teach patrons how to use different technological tools to help with their creative writing projects.

Educational Events

The final type of event that is often successful during the summer is an educational event. An event of this type offers patrons the opportunity to pick up specific skills or to learn about topics of special interest or importance to them. Specific suggestions are described in this section.

Cooking Classes

Many library users like to borrow cookbooks to help them learn to make new recipes. During the summer months, when many of your adult patrons may be reading cookbooks as part of their summer reading challenge, you can capitalize upon their interest in recipes by offering a cooking class. Library cooking classes are a great way to attract cookbook readers to events, and they also provide a perfect opportunity to highlight some of the little-known books of your cookbook collection. Cooking classes can also connect easily to your summer reading theme. The connection can be as simple as preparing recipes inspired by works of literature or as complex as organizing an entire class around the summer reading theme.

To get started planning a cooking class for your summer reading program, first identify individuals in your community who might have the talent and availability to present such a class. These may include chefs from area restaurants, students or faculty at culinary schools, local television or radio personalities, or even residents who cook for fun but have reputations for making excellent dishes.

Once you have an instructor in mind, consider the logistics of cooking in the library. Focus on the following areas:

- Cooking equipment. Does your library have a kitchen? If so, is it large enough to accommodate a chef and his or her audience? If not, are you able to provide portable cooking equipment or to accommodate equipment brought in by your instructor?
- Ingredients. Be sure to work out with the instructor who will pay for the ingredients for the planned dish and how they will be purchased. If the library is responsible for acquiring and storing ingredients, confirm as soon as possible that library staff knows where and how to purchase these items and that you have the appropriate space to store what is needed.
- Space. Libraries with larger spaces might be able to host a class where participants prepare dishes right alongside the instructor. Others might only be able to host a demonstration, where the instructor prepares a dish in front of an audience, as might happen on a cooking show on television. Depending on fire codes and other building ordinances, you also may only be permitted to cook in certain areas of the library.
- Allergies. Some of your patrons are likely to have food allergies. To avoid potential allergy-related problems, encourage your presenter to choose dishes that do not contain common allergens. Also make sure to clearly state on all promotional materials which dish will be prepared and the ingredients involved. This way individuals with allergies can determine whether they can safely participate.

Armchair Travel Lectures

Like cookbooks, travel books are another popular genre among many adult library patrons. If your summer reading bingo card or checklist includes a travel category, or if travel, culture, or vacation is a part of your summer reading theme, an "armchair travel" presentation can be a great addition to your program for adults.

A high-quality armchair travel lecture is more than just an individual sharing his or her vacation photos and itinerary. The presenter you hire should have a good story to tell to accompany his or her photos and experiences. Local travel writers, journalists, and photographers all make great hosts for these events because they have often traveled to different locations and witnessed interesting natural phenomena or historical events.

When you host an armchair travel presentation, be sure to allow time for questions and answers so that patrons can have the opportunity to gain as much knowledge as possible from the presenter. Also be sure to display travel books and works of fiction connected with the region on which the lecture focuses so that patrons can explore the topic further on their own and so that they become aware of all that the library's collection includes.

Genealogy Workshop

Another popular reason many people visit libraries is to conduct genealogical research on their own families. Though genealogy books might not be the kind of thing your patrons read for summer recreation, the idea of tracing personal histories can connect to a variety of summer reading themes, including history, technology, community, storytelling, trees (as in family trees), and even mysteries. Offering a genealogy workshop is not only a great way to reach a specific portion of your patron base during the summer, but it also provides an opportunity to increase usage statistics for any genealogical tools your library offers and to minimize your patrons' frustrations in pursuing their interest in tracing their ancestry.

If a member of the library's staff is an expert on conducting genealogical research, it makes sense for this individual to conduct the workshop. If no one on the staff feels confident in teaching patrons about genealogy, reach out to other area librarians (both public and academic), history departments at high schools and colleges, historical societies, and local authors who write history texts to find experts in your area. Use the workshop to walk patrons through the process of searching different databases to find their ancestors, then address the specific needs of individual patrons as time allows. If you have many patrons who are interested in recording their family histories for posterity, you can follow up with an additional event about memoir writing and/or preserving important personal documents.

Informational Seminars

Adult patrons frequently have concerns about particular problems and situations that are unique to their stage in life. As you plan your summer events, consider addressing some of these by inviting representatives from local businesses and community organizations to answer common questions and troubleshoot specific concerns in a seminar format. Potential topics include

- College applications
- Elder care and end-of-life planning
- Financial aid
- Financial planning
- Résumés and job applications
- Retirement planning

Informational seminars can be a great way to connect local organizations with individuals who need their help but do not know whom to ask. Hosting a seminar of this type also opens a line of communication between the library and these community organizations so that staff are better equipped to answer future questions as they arise and so that they know exactly where to refer a patron for more-detailed information.

◎ Key Points

This chapter has outlined many possible ways to make adult summer reading a success at your library.

- Including adults in summer reading allows you to fulfill your library's mission statement, encourage families to visit the library together, meet your patrons, build community, and promote your collection.
- Attract adult participants to your program by planning a well-organized program, reaching out to regular library users, and partnering with community groups.
- Reading and reporting methods for adults should be challenging but straightforward. Reading logs, bingo cards, and checklists work best.
- Rewards are not absolutely necessary for adult summer reading program participants, but many libraries do choose to do giveaways or to host a celebration for patrons at the end of the summer.
- As you plan summer reading events for adults, it is helpful to consider several key programming areas: reading, community, technology, arts, and education.

Now that you have become familiar with best practices for creating summer reading programs for each age group, the next chapter will help you determine the best methods for promoting your program to the public.

Promoting Your Summer Reading Program

ONCE YOU HAVE DECIDED WHAT TYPE OF SUMMER READING PROGRAM you will offer and whom you will ask to participate, it is important to begin promoting the program as soon as you can. There are many effective ways to do this. As you decide how and where to advertise, consider the benefits and logistics of each of the options named in this chapter: print materials, media outlets, social media, library website, neighborhood email lists, and school visits.

Print Materials

Printed advertisements posted in your library and distributed to patrons at public desks are probably the most common way that libraries promote their summer reading programs. If your patrons are already accustomed to picking up printed promotional materials to find out about programs, then definitely continue to use this method as you begin to promote summer reading.

Because summer reading programs involve a lot of information—dates and times of events, rules for signing up and completing the program, details about rewards and prizes, and so on—it is very important to organize your printed materials well. If your library offers programs for multiple age groups, the best approach is to create one printed flyer (two-sided or brochure style, if necessary) for each age bracket that includes information only for that audience. This makes it easy for patrons of all ages to identify the information that pertains to them, or to the children in their care, and avoids any confusion that might be caused by having to wade through irrelevant details to find what they really need to know. Make it very clear at the top of each printed page who the target audience is for that flyer so that patrons can identify it at a glance. Rather than classifying the age groups by team name or another designation that would only make sense to someone already "in the know," keep it simple and state the specific age range only. There will be room further down the flyer for the more theme-specific embellishments.

Printed materials must also always include the library's name and contact information in an easy-to-find location. Often patrons will pick up a flyer with the understanding that they can always find out more later on. Make it easy for them to do so by listing your library's phone number, email address, website, social media accounts, and, if you can, the name and direct contact information for the person in charge of the specific program being advertised. This way patrons who realize when they get home that they forgot to get clarification for something can easily follow up. Without a way to contact your library, confused patrons can easily decide to simply forget participating altogether. Placing contact information on your printed materials also makes it easy for you to send them to other organizations, knowing that individuals who receive them from other agencies will know how to reach you if they are interested in the program.

In terms of formatting, make sure to use a font size that is large enough to be read by your patrons, and avoid overly busy fonts that can make it difficult to read your words. If you print in color, use color combinations that are pleasing to the eye and make it easy to read what you have printed. Use headings to differentiate between sections and bullet points to separate key pieces of information. When listing events, use a consistent format for the name of each event, the date and time it will be held, and its planned location.

In addition to flyers promoting specific programs, also be sure to print simple signs to hang up around your library letting patrons know that summer reading programs are available and when and where they should sign up. Because patrons are notorious for not reading signs, place them in strategic locations where patrons cannot help but look, such as inside the doorways of bathroom stalls, on the entrance and exit doors of your library building, and near computer sign-in stations. To further catch patrons' attention, consider printing bookmarks, magnets, or buttons to hand out when they borrow items. Those who do not read signs often become more interested when the information is printed on a free handout.

Another option is to print door hangers bearing your library's summer reading information and canvas neighborhoods in your library's service area. Patrons will be less likely to ignore information if it is hanging on their front doors, and by reaching out to all community members, not just those with library cards, you spread awareness of your program to as many potential participants as possible, including those who may not even realize there is a library nearby.

BRANDING

A major part of promoting your summer reading program is creating a brand that represents the goals of the program and the people you wish to have participate. If you use a theme, it is very easy to turn that into your brand. Even if you have a themeless program, however, you will still want all of your promotional materials to work together in projecting a particular image of your program.

As you create print materials, T-shirts, bulletin board designs, video announcements, and other types of advertisements, you can effectively brand these items by paying attention to the fonts, graphics, and colors that you use. By coordinating these three features of each item you produce, you create a professional-looking set of promotional materials that give patrons a positive impression of your library and its summer programming. Branding also makes it easy for patrons to differentiate your summer reading program material from any other promotional materials you have available at your public desks and for them to recognize your materials when they encounter them outside of the library.

Library Website

It is likely that your library's website is your community's main source of information about the programs, events, and materials you offer. Accessing your website is also the first way many new library users and members of local media will encounter your library. Therefore, it is absolutely essential that you post summer reading information prominently on the website as soon as it is available and keep the details up to date all summer long.

To make sure this task is easy to complete and that users can access everything they need to know about summer reading in a number of different ways, use these strategies:

1. Have a dedicated summer reading page on your website, and link to it from the home page. (If your website has an image carousel on its home page, also make sure the link is featured there for the duration of the summer reading program.) When the summer reading page is always available, users are reminded of summer reading each time they visit your library's website. A dedicated page for summer reading also allows you to post all the details about your program—with links to registration forms, event calendars, and sponsors' websites—in one place. Your summer reading webpage can also be redesigned each year to represent the year's theme and brand without interfering with the rest of your site.

2. Promote your library's social media accounts on the home page. Your patrons may only visit your website once or twice, but they most likely log in to their favorite social media sites daily. By having links to your accounts readily available on your website, you increase the chance of connecting with your website visitors again on a site they visit often. Then when you share summer reading information on social media, those individuals who first found your library using Google are kept up to date as well.

3. Identify summer reading events on your calendar. When library patrons are seeking out information on summer reading from a library's website, one of the first places they look is at the events calendar. Make it easy for these patrons to find your sum-

mer reading events by labeling or tagging them as such. Also include the first day of registration and the last day to pick up prizes as individual events so that patrons become aware of the reading and tracking component of your program.

4. Write up blurbs about summer reading. To keep website visitors interested in your summer reading program, post a variety of updates throughout the summer. Highlight individual events for different age groups, or interview some of your participants about their enjoyment of summer reading. Announce and congratulate winners, praise schools whose students participate heavily, and share book recommendations. Posting these updates throughout the summer helps patrons develop a sense of summer reading as an exciting and ongoing event.

Social Media

Social media is becoming a more and more popular way for patrons of all ages and backgrounds to communicate and stay informed, and new applications seem to appear every few months. This section will address best practices for using the most common applications available now; many of these should also be applicable to newer types of social media that are developed in the future.

Facebook

There are two main ways you can use Facebook to promote your summer reading program. You can post announcements, reminders, and events to your library's own Facebook page and encourage patrons to find and follow you. Additionally, you can join Facebook groups your patrons might already be in and reach out to them on their own turf. Both methods have definite benefits and drawbacks, which you will have to weigh as you determine how you will use Facebook in your promotional efforts.

Facebook Pages

A library Facebook page is really only a useful promotional tool if you use it frequently, making regular posts of interest to your patrons even when you are not looking to advertise the summer reading program. Facebook uses a particular algorithm to determine which of your followers see any given post that you make, and this formula seems to favor your content more heavily if you are active on a regular basis. Therefore, if you plan to use social media to promote summer reading in a given year, be sure to start building your Facebook following well in advance. This will include posting signs in the library announcing your Facebook page, reminding patrons about your Facebook page any time you interact with them, and promoting your Facebook page in any newsletter, email list, or social media account you already use to disseminate library news.

Ensuring that content regularly appears on your Facebook page will also involve creating a posting schedule for your staff to use so that a post is made each day, or however often you deem appropriate. Facebook does have a function for scheduling posts in advance, so even if you can only devote time to it once a week, you should still be able to schedule one daily post without taking too much time away from other duties. Another option is to ask a volunteer or member of your Friends group to contribute to the library by taking on this task for you.

Whether a staff member or volunteer posts to Facebook on behalf of the library, the responsible party should follow these strategies in order to maximize the number of people who see your posts:

- Include images. Images are more obvious to users' eyes as they scan down their Facebook news feeds, and they are more likely to be shared to others' pages and groups, especially if there is something familiar, humorous, "cute," or controversial about them. While you want to avoid offending your patrons using the very medium you wish to use to endear them to the library, it can be appropriate to post graphics showing thought-provoking quotations, funny cartoons and "memes," and news items pertaining to literature, reading, and libraries. You can also post photos of the library building, members of the staff, patrons (if they give permission), and library events to entice community members to come in and visit. When it comes time to promote summer reading itself, these images can also include photos of your summer reading bulletin boards, flyers, brochures, and schedules. You can even create digital flyers to promote specific events and important dates.
- Be brief. Social media users are generally not looking to read lengthy posts when they check their Facebook feeds. Try not to lose their interest by posting long descriptions with too many details. When sharing content in order to build a following, a sentence or two to engage the reader with the image you have posted is more than enough. Sometimes, in fact, no words are necessary at all. When publishing a promotional post, it is enough to include just the basic details about your program with a link to more information on your library's website. It is occasionally okay to be a bit more wordy, but this should be an exception used to gain extra attention from your regular followers rather than a consistent habit.
- Use tags. In any Facebook post, you have the ability to "tag" another page or user. By tagging the Facebook pages of community organizations, authors, and specific book titles in your posts, you may attract Facebook users who already follow those pages and encourage them to follow yours. For summer reading–specific posts, you might tag local schools who have provided book lists, paid performers who might give presentations in your library, local organizations that have donated prizes or funding for your program, and Friends groups that have contributed to your program. When using tags, be aware that other pages and users will be notified when you include a tag, and try not to spam them by tagging the same ones all the time. Also try to avoid tagging a personal account for someone who also has a public page, as many people like to keep their private lives separate from their professional Facebook activities.

Facebook Groups

If you would prefer to avoid all the work of keeping up with a Facebook page for your library itself but you still want to benefit somehow from the power of this social networking tool, it might be a better option for you to promote your programs in Facebook groups. Many community organizations choose to connect on Facebook rather than setting up their own email lists or forums. Examples of the kinds of organizations that might meet virtually on Facebook are parent/teacher organizations, parenting support groups, civic groups (Lions Club, Rotary, Kiwanis, etc.), and local interest groups brought together by common hobbies.

Not all of these groups are guaranteed to welcome new members or to allow promotional posts. Indeed, many Facebook groups have very stringent guidelines put in place by no-nonsense administrators whose approval is required before you can join. Therefore, before you start clicking to join a whole series of Facebook groups, it is wise to do a bit of research and networking.

First, think about organizations with involved members you already know. Could one of your contacts vouch for you with the group administrator? Is there someone in your network who is in charge of his or her organization's Facebook group? If so, let those contacts know of your interest in occasionally sharing library events in their groups' forums and see if they might be willing to invite you to join. If you do not have any contacts in any of the groups you wish to join, take a look at the public information about each one. If the rules seem fairly relaxed and it looks as though promotional posts about community events are welcome, it is probably fine to request to join. (In some cases, groups like this may even have open membership.) If there are no rules listed or you feel unsure, you can send a direct message to the group administrator presenting your reasons for wanting to join and your intentions once you gain membership.

Once you have joined the group, be sure not to abuse the privilege of your membership. Keep your promotional posts to just a few occasional reminders, and always follow the rules about how often you are allowed to post and what types of images are allowed. When engaging with other users, maintain a professional attitude, just as you would with a patron on your telephone or at your desk, and always remember that even if you are posting under your own name, you are representing the library in that particular setting.

Twitter

Compared with Facebook, Twitter is a much busier social media application. Conversations on Twitter can be fast paced and difficult to follow, owing in part to the 280-character limit on tweets, which often requires users to put forth many short posts to make a single point. To help your library's account stand out amid the constant chatter, you should definitely establish a username that is directly related to your library's name. Since usernames are limited to fifteen characters, you will need to be a little bit creative and abbreviate your library's full name. There is also a fifty-character space for you to insert a name, plus additional space for a short biography, so between those two elements, you should be able to make your identity clear enough to those who will be looking to connect with your library.

Though it might be helpful to build up a following on Twitter, it is even more useful to make good use of hashtags. Hashtags are user-created categories that help to organize different types of content. To associate a tweet with a hashtag, you type a hash symbol (#) followed by a word or phrase suggesting what your tweet is about. Examples of commonly used hashtags in the library field are "#library," "#librarian," and "#storytime."

If you want to use Twitter to promote your summer reading program and to interact with participants throughout the summer, it is a good idea to establish a unique hashtag to group all tweets about your summer reading program together. As you consider what you might like to use for a hashtag and begin to use it in your tweets, remember these rules of thumb:

- Be specific. A general hashtag like "#SummerReading" or "#SummerReadingProgram" is easy to remember, but it is also likely to be used by many Twitter users and not just those affiliated with your library. A hashtag combining these general ideas with the name of your specific library or city is much more effective because others are not likely to use it, and therefore there will not be any extra tweets to confuse users wanting to talk about your specific program. If you worked for the Anytown Public Library, for example, you might begin tagging your posts using "#Anytown-SummerReading," "#APLSummerReading," or "#SummerReadingAnytownPL."

- Be unique. Before you begin using a hashtag, search Twitter to see if it is already being used regularly by other accounts. If there is already a library or other group tweeting with your chosen hashtag, consider modifying it slightly to make your tweets distinct. If the hashtag has been used in the past (a year ago or more) but no longer seems to be active, there should be no problem with you adopting it as your own.

- Be brief. Twitter does not place any particular character limit on hashtags, but you still want yours to be short enough so that you can fit some substantive text into your tweet alongside it. Typically, a two- or three-word phrase is sufficient.

- Share your hashtag. In addition to using the hashtag on your tweets, you also want to make it possible for your teen and adult patrons who might use Twitter to add it to their tweets. To make it easy for them to find, identify your preferred hashtag on your library's website, on in-library signage, and on any printed material you hand out to promote summer reading.

- Acknowledge others' tweets marked with your hashtag. To encourage your patrons to use the hashtag to keep in touch with you throughout the summer, demonstrate to them that library staff are interested in what they have to say by acknowledging their tweets. You can do this by replying to their tweets to strike up a conversation, retweeting their posts to share with your followers, or clicking the heart symbol beneath their tweets to "like" them.

Instagram

Instagram is a social media application for sharing photos and short videos and can be used by any library with access to a smartphone. Much like Twitter, Instagram allows you to build up a following but also groups posts according to hashtags so that users who do not follow you will often still see what you post. Unlike Twitter, however, Instagram does not place a character limit on posts, so you are free to include as much text as you would like. Instagram is also similar to Facebook in that you can tag individual users in your posts.

As you kick off your summer reading program, you can share photos of your library's flyers, prizes, game boards, bulletin boards, and displays in order to entice patrons to sign up. With each photo, include some text that invites your followers to participate and provides specific details about upcoming events, including when and where to attend and how to contact the library directly for further information. Also accompany each of these posts with the hashtag you have created for your summer reading program and any other hashtags that might help members of your community find your account. Hashtags will vary from community to community, but a Google search for "Instagram hashtags" and the name of your city, town, or county will usually lead you to many options. You can also click on individual hashtags within Instagram itself to see suggestions of others to use for the same type of subject matter. Each Instagram post is allowed to include up to thirty hashtags.

You can also use Instagram to keep patrons engaged in your program throughout the summer by sharing photos of happenings at your library. These might include special performances, story times, participants reading in the library, or the distribution of prizes to those who have completed summer reading. When you post photos of this type, also be sure to include some text that explains what is shown in the photo, as well as your summer reading hashtags. If your photos feature a particular community partner or paid performer, do a search on Instagram to find out if that individual has an account and tag that person in the post as well.

Meetup

Meetup is a networking site for adults that helps users with similar interests find one another virtually so they can get together (or "meet up") in person to pursue their common goals, interests, and hobbies. For libraries, Meetup can be a wonderful way to draw in new

SHARING PHOTOS OF YOUR PATRONS ON SOCIAL MEDIA

Most social media applications allow you to include photos with your posts. Though it might be tempting to post every photo you take, it is important that you only publish images of patrons when they have given their consent. There are two main ways to ensure that you have permission to post your patron's photo.

The first approach is to only photograph individuals who have given you their express permission. If you choose to have patrons opt in to the opportunity to have their photo posted online, you will need to have photo release forms available at every summer reading event you offer and have a system for organizing and saving them. This also means that you cannot use a photo on your library's social media account unless everyone shown in it has granted their permission or had permission granted by a parent or caregiver on their behalf. This approach can become tedious if you take many photos or have very popularly attended events, but it is often preferred by administrators who are concerned about negative responses from the community.

The second approach, which is being adopted by more and more libraries, is to ask those patrons who do not wish to have their photos (or their children's photos) appear online to opt out. This method requires you to publicize as much as you can that attendance at library events implies consent to be photographed unless the patron voices an objection. To be thorough, include this information on event flyers, online posts about the events, and on signs posted during the event. In general, the number of people who object to being photographed is significantly smaller than the number of those who do not mind, so it is typically easier for a library to keep track of who does not wish to have their picture published.

Whichever method you use, it is important to be mindful of protecting your patrons' privacy online. When you do post photos of patrons, avoid including any personally identifying information, such as their last name, birth date, or address, and respond quickly to any individual who requests to have her or his photo taken down.

users with engaging programs like summer reading. Here are the steps you need to take to use Meetup to promote your summer reading events:

1. Pay to create a group on the Meetup site. Unlike individuals, who use the site free of charge, groups are charged a monthly fee for use of the Meetup platform. The fee is $9.99 per month for groups with up to fifty members and four organizers ("Basic"), and $14.99 per month for unlimited membership and unlimited organizers ("Unlimited"). If your adult summer reading program is new, you are not likely to need more than the Basic option; if this is simply a new way of promoting an existing program, choose between Basic and Unlimited based on your typical past attendance. There is a one-month free trial available, so you can try the site without being charged before you commit to using it continually.

2. Identify the topics your group focuses on. Before you even give your group a name, the Meetup website will prompt you to identify your group's main interests. By typing in a keyword, such as "library," you will generate a series of headings related to the keyword. Select as many of these as apply to your group. Also try keywords and phrases like "summer reading," "book clubs," and "reading" to get some more ideas for where your group might fit. It is important to select as many relevant categories as possible, as users browsing Meetup will see your group listed under each topic that you select, thus maximizing your exposure.

3. Give your group a name. Names on Meetup tend to be very straightforward so that users of the site can easily find others with similar interests without much guesswork. If you are only using your Meetup group for summer reading, your name can be something as simple as "Summer Reading at the Anytown Public Library." If you think you may want to use the group for other programs during the year, you can make the name broader, such as "Anytown Public Library's Adult Department" or "Programs for Adults at Anytown Public Library." Avoid generic names that leave out the name of your library or the specific focus of the group, as these will be more likely to be passed over by potential members.

4. Describe your group. At the same registration step where you give your group a name, you are also asked to provide a description. Like your group name, this should be simple and direct and not necessarily a full listing of all the requirements of your summer reading program. Three or four sentences describing the basics of your summer reading program, with an invitation to learn more, should be sufficient to entice potential participants.

5. Post summer reading events. Once you have your group set up, any individual who is designated as an organizer can log in and add events to your group's calendar. As you add events, you have the option of limiting attendance to a certain number of participants, which can be helpful when you have limited space. Meetup also encourages group members to RSVP to each event, which can help you plan ahead for events where you might need to purchase food or other items for distribution to attendees. It is also possible to issue users tickets that they must present upon arrival to your event, and using the smartphone app, you can even take attendance for each event, instantly recording your statistics for later access.

6. Make announcements using the email list. Each Meetup group is also an email list. Even if you do not have many events during your summer reading program, having participants sign up for your Meetup group gives you a way to communicate with them about your program in a more direct and personal way than your

typical library newsletter. Use this feature to remind members of the start and end date of your program and to communicate information about accessing book lists, picking up prizes, and any last-minute changes to your events calendar. You can also use the email list to facilitate book discussions and encourage patrons to get to know one another.

Meetup is a great way to promote your library's adult summer reading program to people who may not otherwise be aware of it or who might not even use your library yet. Since many of your patrons are probably already using Meetup to find events of interest, they might find it easier to connect with your library through an already-familiar means rather than having to add a new social media application to their routine.

YouTube

As online video streaming becomes more and more popular, YouTube does as well. This site allows users to upload and share their personal videos with the world. By signing up for a YouTube account in your library's name, you establish yet another means of connecting with your patrons on a site they use regularly. There are four main ways to use YouTube to promote your summer reading program:

- Public service announcements. Each year, the Collaborative Summer Library Program (CSLP) develops a set of public service announcements (PSAs) to promote the summer reading program. These can be downloaded from the CSLP website (www.cslpreads.org) and uploaded to individual library YouTube channels. Many libraries also choose to film and upload their own promotional videos, starring members of their staff, Friends groups, or teen advisory boards. These PSAs can be as simple or elaborate as your budget, time, and resources allow, as long as they inform patrons about summer reading and endeavor to get them interested in joining.
- Video presentations for schools. Later in this chapter, you will learn about using school visits to promote your summer reading programs for kids and teens. Sometimes, though, it is not possible for you to visit a particular class, grade level, or school building, in which case you can record your presentation to be played for the students in your absence. Though some schools may not allow videos from YouTube to be played on their school networks, having the presentation available on YouTube affords parents the opportunity to hear the information firsthand.
- Video book talks. Another great way to use YouTube during summer reading is to suggest great titles to your patrons. Members of the staff can give their recommendations, or you can invite patrons to guest star in your videos with their own recommended reads. These videos are especially useful because they can continue to engage patrons online even after summer reading is over, for as long as the books mentioned are on the library's shelves.
- Recordings of summer reading events. Finally, the best way to get patrons excited about summer reading is to show them how much fun it is. By recording videos of your summer reading events and sharing the highlights to YouTube, you can show patrons rather than tell them what the summer reading program is really like. Sharing videos of events as they happen is helpful, as is reflecting on the fun of past summers in order to build anticipation for what you might do next year.

YouTube is one social media outlet that is used by all ages. Elementary school kids and teens are as savvy in their use of the site as their parents and grandparents, so it is a great way to reach everyone using a familiar and fun means.

Media Outlets

In-house and web-based promotional tools are useful for reaching individuals who are already aware of your library, but if you want to disseminate summer reading information to the larger community, local media outlets can be very helpful. As the start of your summer reading program approaches, consider which local radio and TV stations and which newspapers and magazines published in your community might be most helpful in spreading the word.

At the very least, issue a press release to each of these outlets so that the pertinent information about summer reading can be included in the local news. If you care to use these outlets in a stronger capacity, you might also consider having a staff person give an interview, either in print or on the air, to tell patrons about summer reading. You can also purchase advertising spots, submit your PSAs, and ask for reporters to cover some of your main summer reading events. Local media might also be interested in running stories about patrons who have completed summer reading.

Before contacting members of the local media, always be aware of your library's policies on media interaction. If there is an individual (or department) in charge of marketing for your library, speak with that person first. Larger libraries' marketing departments in particular might already have relationships with media contacts in place, and they may prefer that you allow them to set up any discussions or meetings.

Neighborhood Email Lists

In many communities, and especially in urban areas, a great way to reach out to potential summer reading participants is through neighborhood email lists. Typically, these are lists moderated by average citizens that help members of the community share events and information pertaining to their immediate surroundings. Ask around your library's neighborhood or use Google to help you find any active email lists, then request to join those that seem most likely to include potential summer reading participants. As with a Facebook group, be sure to observe any rules and norms the email list has established for promoting events, and avoid spamming other members of the list with an overwhelming number of posts. For example, instead of posting about each individual event as it happens, send out a single message letting the list know about summer reading, with a link to the details on your website. Also, always include your contact information so that interested list members can contact you off-list for more information without cluttering the email list itself.

Another important thing to remember when using email lists is that even when others are casual and candid, you are still a representative of the library. This means you should maintain your professionalism even when list members may happen to make negative comments about your summer reading program or even your library in general. While these types of posts might feel personal, usually the individuals who make them are just venting to their neighbors, and they are not necessarily even aware that you are reading them. Though it might be tempting to join the conversation and defend your library, it is a better approach to simply provide summer reading information to those who will appreciate it and otherwise remain a silent observer of the list's activities.

School Visits

For children's and teen librarians, outreach visits to schools are a key component of promoting summer reading programs. While other methods of promotion reach out to parents, school visits are a way to engage kids directly and get them interested in summer reading even if your programs are not yet on their parents' radars. This section will cover some of the challenges librarians face when collaborating with schools, as well as best practices to put in place during your actual visits.

Scheduling Your School Visit

The first hurdle you will need to overcome in planning these important school visits is the problem of scheduling them with your local schools. From a librarian's point of view, it is best to have these visits occur as close to the start of the summer reading program as possible. Unfortunately, summer reading typically begins just as school ends, and the last few weeks of the school year are among the most hectic. Between standardized tests, moving up ceremonies, band concerts, and other end-of-the-year traditions, it can be really difficult for a school to find a good time for a librarian to come in for a visit. This is not an insurmountable problem, however, as long as you plan ahead.

While there is no guarantee that a school will be able to accommodate you at all, it is more likely that you will have the chance to see students if you contact the schools well in advance. Sometime between the end of winter break and the start of the final semester, quarter, or trimester, reach out to the school community with your offer to make a presentation for students about the summer reading program. If possible, approach a contact person who can help you coordinate with multiple grade levels and classes rather than individual classroom teachers. A school library media specialist is often very helpful in this capacity, but a principal, assistant principal, or even an English teacher might also be interested, especially if the school gives summer reading assignments. Be as flexible as you can with scheduling, and make it clear that students are welcome to visit you at the library if that is more convenient. Then as soon as the school is prepared to make a schedule, nail down specific dates and put them in writing.

Making Time for School Visits

Another serious challenge facing many libraries is finding the time to visit schools amid a librarian's many other commitments. If you have the opportunity to visit schools, however, it is important to find a way to make it work, as meeting with kids and teens face-to-face can be a great boon to your summer reading program. If you are having trouble figuring out how to fit school visits into your regular schedule, try some of these strategies:

- Arrange to give an assembly to an entire student body at one time rather than visiting each grade or classroom. This way you only have to be absent from the library for one session per school and you still reach every child or teen.

- Invite classes to visit you at the library. You can cut down on the time it takes to travel to schools and set up your presentation by having students visit you on your own turf. This way you can transition right into desk duty or whatever other task requires your attention upon the conclusion of your summer reading presentation. Alternatively, you could also provide your presentation over Skype or another video-networking tool, which would allow you to remain at the library and connect with your audience virtually.
- Cancel in-house events during school visit season. If all of your school visits are scheduled during a specific time frame, such as the month of April or the first two weeks of May, consider scheduling a break from story times and other events that normally occur during the school day to accommodate your visits to the schools.
- Record your summer reading presentation. If you truly cannot get away from the library to visit all of the schools in your community, you can record yourself giving a short, age-appropriate talk about summer reading and distribute it to the schools electronically. Individual teachers can then show the video to their students at a convenient time and provide your contact information for kids who want to get in touch.

In many communities, promoting summer reading programs is the only thing that gets a public librarian into a school at all. It is important not to miss this golden opportunity to entice kids to start using the library and hopefully to continue to use it after summer ends.

Planning for School Visits

The format you use for your school visit will be determined primarily by the age of the students you will encounter. As you plan how and what you will share with students on your visits, you will need to consider their developmental needs, attention spans, and interests, along with other important factors like the size of your audience and the space and time provided to you by the school.

Preschool to Grade 2

For younger children in the preschool and early elementary years, it is typical to present a story time as part of the summer reading presentation. Reading books (or telling stories, if groups are too large for a traditional read-aloud) related to the summer theme, or about libraries in general, makes a great jumping-off point for explaining the summer reading program and getting kids excited to participate. Though you can certainly tell children in this age group about your program and encourage them to sign up, most of them will probably not be able to relay the message correctly to their parents when they go home later in the day. Therefore, it is essential for you to provide the children with something tangible to bring to their parents. The simplest thing to do is bring along a stack of summer reading flyers explaining your early childhood program and have the classroom teachers send them home. Many classrooms have a particular day of the week on which important correspondence goes home with children, so it is helpful to find out when that is and plan accordingly. If the teachers regularly email parents and you wish to conserve paper, consider emailing a PDF version of the flyer ahead of time so that it can be forwarded easily. Another option is to send the children home with something that will also excite them, such as a bookmark or sticker, which will be seen by the parent and then used by the child.

If your presentation time slot is not long enough for a story time, or if you would just prefer a different approach, a summer reading school visit is also a great time to teach little ones about libraries and the people who work in them. Prepare a short lesson with interactive elements such as guessing games or age-appropriate library trivia questions, which will help children more fully understand what a library is for, and then segue into talking about summer reading. Preschoolers and kindergartners love to ask questions, so depending on how much time you have, you may be able to fill the entire session just by answering questions on what they would like to know about libraries.

Grades 3 to 6

For older kids, starting around third grade, the presentation can be more of a discussion where the librarian asks the students questions and vice versa. It is also common to include book talks in these sessions, where you highlight some of the new exciting titles you hope summer reading participants will enjoy. Elementary-aged students often respond well to prizes, so if you do have something up for grabs for completing the program, bring a prototype along with you.

Elementary schools are also great places to get a bit more creative with your presentations. Skits, puppet shows, guessing games, jokes, musical performances, and other interactive approaches work well with school-age kids, and they give you a chance to show your enthusiasm for summer reading and demonstrate the library's fun approach to reading.

Grades 7 to 12

Middle school and high school students will enjoy many of the same approaches you take with younger students: presenting book talks, playing trivia games, and showing off potential prizes. Slightly more sophisticated versions of these will work nicely when you address groups during class, in the school library, or in a larger assembly. Often, though, as an alternative to an assembly, schools invite librarians to set up tables in the library, cafeteria, or another prominent area of the school to speak one-on-one with students about summer reading.

Since you do not have a captive audience in this situation, you may need to get more creative about engaging students, as you can only tell them about summer reading if they agree to talk to you in the first place. To get kids interested, make sure to sit where they must walk past you. If it is easy to avoid you, many teens will do so, especially if they have other things on their minds and do not know who you are. Make your table look as interesting as possible, with lots of teen-friendly flyers, freebies to give away, and books on a variety of topics and make a point of speaking to students first, giving a quick, friendly greeting followed by a brief mention of why you are visiting the school. Most of all, display your social media account names. Kids who are interested might not want to talk to you during school but will gladly get in touch later on. Though it is most desirable to meet with students in a group setting in the hopes of allowing everyone to hear about your summer reading program, an assertive approach to tabling can also prove fruitful.

🌀 Marketing Resources

This chapter's overview of the possibilities for marketing a summer reading program is really only the tip of the iceberg. If you want to improve your promotional strategies or think further outside the box, these great resources can help:

- *Blueprint for Your Library Marketing Plan* by Marseille M. Pride and Patricia H. Fisher (American Library Association, 2011)
- *Crash Course in Marketing for Libraries, 2nd Edition* by Susan Alman and Sara Swanson (Libraries Unlimited, 2014)
- *Creative Library Marketing and Publicity: Best Practices* edited by Robert J. Lackie and M. Sandra Wood (Rowman & Littlefield, 2015)
- *The Library Marketing Toolkit* by Ned Potter (Facet Publishing, 2012)

🌀 Key Points

This chapter has presented you with many options for promoting your summer reading program, which you can adapt as necessary for your own library's needs.

- Use printed materials bearing your library's contact information to promote summer reading both inside and outside of the library.
- Keep your library's website up to date with accurate summer reading information that can be accessed from the home page.
- Reach out to local radio stations, television stations, and print publications to spread summer reading information more widely.
- Engage with patrons on social media sites they already use in order to more effectively inform them about your summer reading programs.
- Join neighborhood email lists to share summer reading information, taking care to always follow each list's rules and norms.
- Children's and teen librarians should plan to visit schools to promote summer reading just before summer vacation begins.
- Seek out resources devoted entirely to library marketing to assist with your specific promotional plans.

Chapter 8 will provide information on evaluating your summer reading program.

Evaluating Your Summer Reading Program

▷ Reflecting on your personal observations and feelings about your summer reading program

▷ Listening to and soliciting feedback about summer reading from participants

▷ Using statistics to draw conclusions about the impact of your summer reading program on your patrons

▷ Summarizing your evaluation findings for use in future years

THE PRECEDING CHAPTERS HAVE GIVEN YOU a strong foundation in the elements that make up successful summer reading programs for different age groups. This chapter will help you think objectively about your program after the fact in order to recognize and celebrate what you have done well and to make adjustments and improvements for future years in order to combat any difficulties you encountered. Specifically, you will learn how to use your personal reactions, community feedback, and program statistics to gain an overall understanding of your summer reading program's success.

Personal Reactions

The most immediate way to know how well your summer reading program has gone is to reflect on your own observations and feelings about the experience. As you implement your program throughout the summer, you gain firsthand knowledge of how your patrons react to each element you introduce. By watching how patrons respond to receiving a reading log, to participating in a given event, or to collecting a prize, you can often gauge how much they have enjoyed the program and how it has enriched their summers. Your interactions with patrons as the program progresses can give you a lot of insight into which elements of your program have been most successful and which need more work.

Similarly, your observations of your fellow staff members are also valuable pieces of information as you begin to evaluate your summer reading program. If staff morale seems low due to stress or staff members are frequently confused or flustered by happenings related to the summer reading program, this can be a sign that there are problems in the program, even if they are not necessarily apparent to the public. Conversely, if staff seem to enjoy the program along with the community, this is a positive sign and an indication that your program is going well.

Along with your observations, your own feelings about the program can also be useful indicators of summer reading success. If your summer has felt stressful, overwhelming, and generally negative, this can be an indication that at least some part of your program has not gone as well as you would have liked. On the other hand, if you have felt energized, enthusiastic, and generally positive for the duration of your program, this can be an indication that things have gone well. Obviously, your emotions are subjective, so it is never a good idea to base your entire evaluation on how you feel. Still, your negative feelings about a particular element of your program can be a great starting point for further investigating what went wrong and how it can be remedied.

◉ Public Feedback

After taking stock of your own feelings about the success of your summer reading program, it is a good idea to find out how these match up with the public's impression of the program. There are three main ways you can gain an understanding of how well your patrons have enjoyed summer reading:

1. Compliments and complaints. Members of the public tend to speak up the most when they are either very pleased about a library program or very disappointed. Whenever you receive a compliment or a complaint during the summer reading program, be sure to make a note of it, either in a specific document you maintain for this purpose or by asking patrons to submit their thoughts in writing on a comment card or web-based form. While single comments in isolation may not indicate anything of significance, a collection of comments might reveal certain trends about areas of your program with which people were or were not completely satisfied.

2. Anecdotes about reading habits. Another useful way to gauge how your summer reading program has impacted your community is to listen to patrons' anecdotes about how their (or their children's) reading habits have changed as a result of their participation. Sometimes patrons share these stories as they happen, letting you know of the husband who never liked to read until he discovered the biography section or the daughter who has finally become motivated to complete her summer reading assignment from school. Other times, these anecdotes trickle in after the summer, as teachers recognize the positive impact your program has had on students or parents begin to see an improvement in their children's grades. Since most libraries do not have direct access to students' reading scores or grades, these anecdotes are often the closest you can get to discovering how your library has reduced summer slide and promoted a love of reading.

3. Surveys. This third method is a more formal way of asking patrons about their summer reading experience. Surveys can be useful for capturing the opinions of those patrons who might not otherwise volunteer their thoughts and for asking about areas of the program about which you have specific concerns. Since summer reading is a program with a definitive ending, you can easily incorporate the survey into your end-of-summer wrap-up activities, asking each participant to take a moment to fill one out. For best results, when you construct your survey, make it possible for patrons to participate anonymously so they feel comfortable giving their honest opinions, and provide both print and online versions of the survey so that patrons can choose how to participate. Also be sure to keep the survey short so it can be filled out quickly, but do leave a space for additional comments the patrons might want to share in case they wish to weigh in on something you have not otherwise mentioned. Figure 8.1 provides a sample of a basic survey that you can customize to suit your needs.

SUMMER READING SURVEY

In which summer reading program(s) did you or your family participate this summer?

Adult   Teen   Children   Early Childhood

How did you and/or your family participate in the summer reading program?
❏ Tracking reading progress
❏ Attending events at the library
❏ Borrowing print reading material from the library
❏ Borrowing digital reading material from the library

How did you learn about the summer reading program?
❏ Library flyer   ❏ Billboard
❏ Library newsletter   ❏ Local newspaper
❏ Library website   ❏ Community email list
❏ Radio advertisement   ❏ Local schools
❏ TV advertisement   ❏ Word of mouth

On a scale of 1–5, please rate the following aspects of this summer's program:

Book lists	1	2	3	4	5
Promotional materials	1	2	3	4	5
Children's events	1	2	3	4	5
Teen events	1	2	3	4	5
Adult events	1	2	3	4	5
Reading logs	1	2	3	4	5
Registration process	1	2	3	4	5
Prizes	1	2	3	4	5

PLEASE SHARE ANY ADDITIONAL FEEDBACK ABOUT THE PROGRAM IN THE SPACE BELOW:

Figure 8.1. Sample Summer Reading Survey. *Created by the author*

⑥ Statistics

After surveys, which formally organize your patrons' opinions of your summer reading program, another way to do a more objective evaluation is to look at the statistics associated with your summer reading program. Typically, there are three types of statistics that you will want to consider: participation in the reading component of the program, attendance at summer reading events, and circulation of materials during the summer months as compared with other times of the year.

Participation

There are a few different numbers that libraries like to track when it comes to collecting participation statistics for the reading component of the summer reading program. Some libraries are only interested in knowing how many summer reading participants completed the program, and they will count those individuals as patrons turn in their finished reading logs, claim their prizes, or earn the required digital badges. Other libraries want to see a comparison between how many patrons registered for the program and how many actually went on to meet the reading goals. These libraries will count patrons both during registration and again at their completion of the program. There are also libraries whose programs include a few benchmarks throughout the summer, and they might keep track of how many participants reach each milestone, as well as how many make it to the end goal.

The numbers that your specific library chooses to track should be directly related to your goals for the program. If your goal, for example, is to close a gap between the number of total registrants and the number of patrons who actually finish the program, it would be important for you to track registrations and completions. If you do not have a specific need for this information, however, there is no need to keep track of statistics for which you have no use. Planning ahead as to which participation statistics will be useful to you can go a long way toward simplifying this aspect of evaluation.

Once you have tallied your participation statistics for a given summer, you can use them to answer a few important questions about the reading component of your program:

- Did the reading contest attract more or fewer participants than in past years?
- Was there a dramatic change in participation as compared with past years?
- Was the expected number of registered readers higher or lower than the actual number?
- Did a particular age group's reading program attract a larger or smaller audience?
- Was there a specific point in the reading contest at which participation seemed to drop off?

By focusing in on questions like these, you can begin to understand where your program fits in the recent history of summer reading at your library and to discover whether your expectations for the next year's program need to be changed. The numbers will fluctuate a bit each year regardless of what you do, but major shifts in participation can sometimes help uncover problems that need to be addressed or changes in community interests and priorities over time.

Circulation

Going hand in hand with participation statistics are statistics related to the circulation of materials during the summer reading program. Since your integrated library system (ILS) should keep track of borrowing statistics automatically, you probably will not need to do anything during the summer months to ensure that you will have this data when the program ends. At the end of the summer, however, librarians should generate reports (or request them from the necessary administrator if they cannot be generated independently) that can provide the following numbers:

- Patrons who registered for new library cards
- Number of materials borrowed by collection (children's, teen, adult, etc.)
- Number of materials borrowed by format (e-books, DVDs, hardcover, etc.)
- Materials with the highest number of checkouts during the summer reading program
- Checkouts for all materials highlighted or used at summer reading events
- Checkouts for all materials listed on library book lists and any school lists to which you have access

Having access to each of these different numbers can help you gain a better understanding of who visited your library during the summer, whether they borrowed books and other materials that were specifically promoted by your events or book lists, and whether there was an overall increase (or decrease) in circulation as compared with other seasons of the year and with previous summers. Being able to study these numbers can also help you answer such questions as:

- Was there a large discrepancy between the number of people who borrowed materials and the number of people who participated in summer reading?
- Was there a particular format that was overwhelmingly popular as compared with others?
- Did a specific age group show a dramatic decrease or increase in the borrowing of materials?
- Did a large number of patrons register for library cards so they could participate in summer reading?
- Was circulation significantly higher during the summer reading program?
- Did promoting specific books seem to increase their circulation?

By answering these questions, you can begin to identify the impact of your summer reading program on the circulation of materials, which can be extrapolated to draw conclusions about the power of your promotional materials, the appeal of the books you promoted during events and on book lists, and whether and how your program encouraged patrons to increase the amount of reading they do.

Attendance

Though summer reading programs always seek to encourage reading, participation in the reading aspect of these programs is only one way in which patrons engage with the library in the summer. Patron attendance at the events you offer is another element you must take into account as you inventory the highs and lows of your summer reading program.

To ensure that you have reasonably accurate attendance statistics for each event that you offer during the summer, it is important to establish a method for tracking this information before the summer even begins. In general, there is no need to track the attendance habits of individual patrons. Rather, your focus should be on assigning a staff member or volunteer to count the total number of people who attend each event and record this number in a place that can be easily accessed at the end of the summer. In some libraries, this may be a tally sheet or calendar kept in a desk drawer or tacked to a bulletin board. In others, statistics may be kept more formally in a spreadsheet or other digitized document.

When counting event participants, use the following guidelines to help you record useful and accurate statistics:

- Count different age groups separately. No matter the intended audience of your event, it is important for you to know who actually attended. For children's programs, count the children who participate, as well as the adults and siblings who accompany them. For adult programs, make note of any children or grandchildren who tag along. Having attendance broken down according to age group helps you see more clearly who visited the library during each event and shows you whether the events you planned truly appealed to the age groups for which you offered them or if the actual audience skewed younger or older.
- Make a note of when classes and camps attend events. To have groups participating in your summer reading events can be a great boon to your overall attendance, but it can sometimes also overwhelm your library and its staff. When you evaluate your program at the end of the summer, it can be helpful to know when large groups such as camps and classes were and were not in attendance at events. If you can, try to count campers and class members separately from the general public, recording a separate statistic for each group. If this proves difficult, simply record the total number of participants and make a note as to which groups came to the event. Later, when you reflect on the success or failure of a particular event, you will be able to see how a group's involvement may have enhanced or detracted from the experience.
- Do not start counting right at the beginning of the event. Library patrons are often late to events. To get an accurate count of the number of people who actually showed up to an event, it is wise to wait at least ten or fifteen minutes before you do your headcount. The true "sweet spot" for counting how many people actually participated in an event is usually the halfway point, after latecomers arrive and before the early departures leave. Waiting this extra time often results in higher attendance counts than you would have if you counted participants at the start of the event and recorded that number.
- Use a tally counter for large audiences. If your summer reading events regularly attract very large audiences, it is worth investing in a tally counter. This handheld device (which is also available as a digital app for iPhones and Android phones from a variety of vendors) allows you to simply click a button each time you count a participant. While staff members can easily count forty to fifty participants without losing track, it becomes increasingly difficult to do so when numbers approach one hundred or more. By stationing someone at the door with a tally counter, you

increase your chances of reaching an accurate total and you limit the possibility of needing to start over when you lose count.

- If you forget to count, it is okay to make an estimate. There may be times when you forget to count the attendees at a particular event. Rather than leaving out the number for this event from your overall statistical report, it is better to make an educated guess about the number of people who participated. Narrow your estimate using helpful guideposts, such as the number of seats in a room (Were they all full? Were half of them full?), the capacity of the room (Was the event at capacity or significantly smaller?), the amount of refreshments consumed, or anything else that might indicate a ballpark number of people who came to the event. Since these statistics are collected largely to help the library in its own efforts to improve summer reading, they do not have to be completely without error in order to be helpful in some way.

After collecting the attendance numbers for individual events all summer long, the resulting data can be helpful in a number of ways. It can help you figure out the popularity of programs of certain types or for certain age groups. It can help you identify the days of the week and times of the day when patrons seemed most likely to attend events. Attendance statistics can also help you figure out which paid performers you might like to hire again, which events might need larger or smaller spaces next year, and even which events you might want to scrap during future programs.

While numbers alone do not tell the whole story about a given event, they do serve as signals to alert you to the highs and lows of your summer event schedule. By reflecting more carefully on those events with very high, very low, or very inconsistent attendance, you will come to a deeper understanding of how they influenced the success of your summer reading program, for better or for worse.

⊚ Summarizing Your Evaluation

When you have had the opportunity to go over all of the data you have collected about your summer reading program, it is important to organize it so that it can be accessed in the future. Though there is often a short period of time of six months or less between the end of one summer reading program and the start of planning for the next one, it is still possible to forget much of what happened or for staff members to leave your library's employment, taking their knowledge of past summers along with them. To ensure that the conclusions you reach as a result of your evaluation are not lost, it is wise to write them up in a report. Though you will probably send statistics to your library system and state library, this report alone is generally not enough to fulfill your in-house needs. While the numbers are useful, your plans for the future, based on the numbers, are what you will need when you sit down to plan your next summer reading program.

When you create your report, therefore, be sure to explicitly record the following:

- Descriptions of any major problems you encountered and your proposed solutions
- Tricks and tips you picked up during the summer that helped the program run more smoothly or eased staff stress
- Notes on paid performers you would or would not wish to hire again, with reasons for your decisions

- Names of camps and groups who participated in summer reading and how their involvement impacted the program overall
- Copies of significant compliments and complaints that will help shape future programs
- Ideas for events and activities that arose during the summer and during the evaluation process

Recording these conclusions not only brings your current summer reading program to a satisfying close, it also provides you with a head start on developing the next summer's program and helps you avoid planning that program completely from scratch.

ⓖ Key Points

This chapter has given you a set of guidelines to help direct your evaluation of your library's summer reading program.

- Use your personal observations and reactions as a starting point for identifying the strengths and weaknesses of your summer reading program.
- Collect patron feedback by listening to compliments, complaints, and anecdotes and by surveying participants for their opinions.
- Record statistics related to summer reading participation, the circulation of materials, and attendance at events in order to identify areas where your program excelled, as well as aspects of the program that may need improvements.
- Write a report of your evaluation findings to be used by those staff members who plan the next summer reading program so that they have a starting point and do not have to start completely from scratch.

This chapter and those preceding it have laid out the process for planning, executing, and evaluating a successful summer reading program. The next chapter will prepare you to face some of the unexpected challenges that may arise in your program when things do not go exactly according to plan.

CHAPTER 9

Solving Summer Reading Problems

▷ Dealing with unexpected logistical problems in your summer reading program

▷ Troubleshooting problems related to summer reading prizes

▷ Handling difficulties associated with hiring paid performers for your summer reading program

▷ Addressing the challenges faced by youth services librarians during summer reading

DESPITE ALL THE CAREFUL PLANNING you put into your library's summer reading program, librarians and patrons are only human, and problems are bound to arise. This final chapter identifies some of the most common difficulties librarians encounter during summer reading and suggests ways to manage these challenges. The problems are presented in question-and-answer format and are sorted by category.

⊚ Planning and Logistics

Even a thoroughly well-thought-out summer reading program hits the occasional bump in the road. This section addresses some of the unexpected problems that may arise during the planning stages or which might interrupt the smooth running of your program as it is implemented.

Some of my patrons go away for the entire summer but still want to participate in summer reading. How can I make this possible?

When one of your goals for summer reading is to increase participation at library events and to attract patrons to your library, it can be frustrating to learn that some of the patrons who have registered for the program will be out of town for much of the summer. While it can be tempting to place limitations on such patrons in order to prevent them from participating, it is better customer service to do your best to accommodate them.

The exact method that will work for your vacationing patrons will differ depending on how your program is structured, but there are three possible ways to have them participate that might ease your frustrations:

1. Have them participate online. If your library offers its summer reading program in a digital format, this is the best way to have patrons participate while they are away from home. By tracking their progress online, your patrons make it possible for you to see how they are progressing so you know whether they are actively participating and can possibly even set aside their prizes to be picked up upon their return. Since other patrons will also be participating using this same method, vacationers' use of the online format also does not add additional responsibilities to a librarian's workload.

2. Ask them to keep in touch. If your library does not yet offer a digital option for tracking summer reading activity, you might still be able to keep reasonable tabs on how your vacationing patrons are progressing through the program by asking them to report to you periodically by email or phone. You may not feel it is necessary to do this, in which case you do not need to offer this option, but if you are concerned about having enough prizes available for these patrons at the end of the summer, this can be a good way to gauge whether you need to set aside prizes for them or not.

3. Find a library in their vacation location. If the in-person elements of your program are so integral that being away makes it impossible for patrons to participate, a third option is to put the patron in touch with a public library in the city where they will spend their summer. This may not work as well for patrons who will be on cruises or traveling abroad, but for those who visit summer homes in other U.S. states, finding a local library with a summer reading program might be preferable to trying to adapt your program to suit their needs. (*Note:* Before you send patrons to another public library, it is a good idea to personally reach out to a librarian at that location and find out the library's policy about guests participating in summer reading.)

Members of my library's staff want to take vacations during summer reading. How can we make this manageable?

Many libraries have adopted policies—either official or unofficial—stating that staff members involved with the summer reading program may never take vacations over the summer. While this might sound like the best way to ensure full staff coverage for summer events, the need for this type of policy is often indicative of a larger problem. Specifically, it suggests that the program you have planned is too much for your library.

To resolve this problem and restore the possibility of summer vacations to your staff, try one of these solutions:

1. Plan your program around staff vacations. While it may feel counterintuitive to put the needs of the library staff above those of your patrons, it is actually one of the best ways to ensure that your program is fully staffed and that staff members are not resentful of a program that prevents them from taking time off. Because

you will need to start the planning process early, this approach also encourages staff to plan their vacations early and to avoid last-minute decisions to miss work. Once you have an established vacation schedule, it is easier to block out certain days as unavailable and others as ideal for hosting events and activities.

2. Only run the summer reading program for part of the summer. Another way to allow for staff vacations during the summer reading program is to run the program for only a portion of the summer—a month, two months, six weeks, and so forth. This makes it possible for staff members to take some time off without having a negative impact on the smooth running of summer reading.

3. Make use of volunteers. While a volunteer can never do all the work of a trained staff member, there are many tasks that can be delegated to reliable volunteers. For example, volunteers might be able to check in with readers and distribute prizes, introduce paid performers, or even run specific activities themselves. If you have capable volunteers at your disposal, there is no reason not to allow them to take on some summer reading tasks in order to make it possible for staff members to be out of the library for a week or two.

Ultimately, it is unreasonable to assume that all library employees associated with summer reading will be willing to give up summer vacations indefinitely. If your summer reading program is so stressful and staff intensive that not a single person can be spared for a single week, it is probably more than your library should reasonably take on.

Many patrons register for my summer reading program but only a fraction of them ever return. How can I encourage everyone to complete the program?

While it is unrealistic to hope that every single person who registers for your summer reading program will complete it, there are some ways to increase the likelihood that registered patrons will return. One way is to make the program as convenient as possible. Offer both print and digital tracking options and make sure deadlines and requirements are listed clearly. Minimize the number of times a patron needs to physically visit the library, and consider offering a grace period for patrons who may miss a deadline. Sometimes the rules of a complicated program can overwhelm patrons who would otherwise happily participate, so simplifying your program in this way may help participants stick with it longer than they would otherwise.

Another way to prevent patrons from dropping out of your program is to issue frequent reminders. Have patrons sign up for email or text reminders and send an alert when deadlines approach. Make announcements at all events about upcoming deadlines and the requirements for completing the program, and keep printable versions of the information on hand for those who may need them. Post signs around the library, especially in bathroom stalls and other places where patrons cannot help but look. While not every patron is going to participate simply because he or she was reminded, providing reminders does make it less likely that a patron who meant to finish the program will simply forget to do so.

Finally, a third way to close the gap between the number of people who register for summer reading and the number who successfully finish the program is to ease up on the pressure you put on patrons to sign up in the first place. Sometimes in their enthusiasm for the program and their desire to maximize the community's participation, librarians persuade individuals to register for summer reading who have no intention of taking part. If patrons are resistant to signing up, they will probably be even more reluctant to read and report their progress. While it is important to make all patrons feel welcome to participate, it is equally important to respect the wishes of those who would prefer to pass and to avoid forcing registrations just to inflate registration statistics.

The summer reading program has been going on for a week and many of my patrons have already completed it. How can I keep them involved for the rest of the summer?

When one of the goals of your summer reading program is to encourage a daily reading habit, it can be especially frustrating to realize that patrons have already finished the program after just a short period of time. While this might seem to you like a flaw in your program, this is not really something you can control, nor is it something to be overly concerned about.

Patrons who finish summer reading early have a variety of reasons for doing so. Some might already be avid readers who report their reading to the library in order to earn a prize and will continue to read all summer with or without a library program to motivate them. Others might quickly complete the program before embarking on a long vacation, going away to summer camp, or starting summer employment. A percentage of early finishers might also just be looking to get the program "out of the way" so they can claim a prize and then immediately stop reading, but even these patrons have the right to work at their own pace rather than at a librarian's preferred pace. The best thing to do is simply congratulate them for completing the program, count them in your statistics, remind them about any upcoming events they might enjoy if they can, and then move on. Any measures you might take to encourage longer or deeper participation in summer reading likely would not change the behaviors of any of these patrons, except perhaps to prevent them from participating at all.

Still, if it seems that patrons are finishing early and wishing there was more for them to do, you can certainly offer a supplemental reading challenge for them. This can be as simple as challenging patrons to read as much as they can before the program ends or as complex as an extra bingo card, checklist, or other reporting tool that can be turned in for an additional prize. If you find it is necessary to offer a supplemental challenge like this each year, it might also be worth considering using an approach to summer reading that requires daily or weekly participation all summer long so that patrons do not need to request a supplement.

Only the members of the summer reading committee at my library seem interested in making the program a success. How can I get other staff members to buy in to the program?

It can be frustrating when it seems that certain staff members or even entire departments within your library do not seem to be on board with your plans for the summer reading program. There are many reasons why you might find it difficult to win them over, but there are some concrete things you can do to make the program less repugnant to staff members who might feel overwhelmed, discouraged, or irritated by your program.

The most important thing you can do is communicate. Often staff members who are not directly involved in planning the summer reading program are reluctant to buy in to it simply because they feel uncertain about the details and therefore lack the confidence to share information accurately with patrons. Taking the time to explain the entire program to them—both in person and in writing so they can refer back to it later—can really make a difference toward how burdensome the program seems and how willingly these staff members will embrace your vision.

It is also important to make sure you check in with staff members repeatedly throughout the summer. This is the best way to find out about problems in your program that you may not recognize yourself and to answer questions that may come up as the weeks wear on. While some staff members might come to you with a major difficulty, others might suffer in silence and even resentment over the fact that you have forced them into assisting patrons with a summer reading program that causes nothing but frustration. Though the summer reading committee is in charge of summer reading, the program itself has to be a team effort of the entire staff, and this can only happen when everyone is on the same page.

The last way to ensure that all staff buy in to your summer reading program is to seek support from your supervisor. Managers can share with staff what their expectations are for involvement with the summer reading program, and they can assist you in communicating the rules and procedures of the program and act as mediators when other staff have frustrations and difficulties.

My library normally uses the Collaborative Summer Library Program (CSLP) theme for summer reading, but this year, we find the selected theme really uninspiring. What should we do?

While many libraries are members of the CSLP (or iRead), there is no hard-and-fast rule that your library must use the provided theme each year. If there is a particular theme that just does not inspire you, consider one of these simple solutions:

- Reinvent the theme. Before you dismiss the entire summer reading theme in one fell swoop, go through the materials and see if there is a particular aspect of the program that would appeal to you. If there is, consider focusing your program on just this aspect of the theme and forgo using the things that you found boring, uninspiring, or disappointing. Sometimes librarians approve of the theme but dislike the artwork provided. In these cases, it is often possible to create your own promotional materials to suit the theme while still using many of the suggested activities.
- Use a past theme. If your library typically uses the CSLP or iRead theme every year, chances are you have materials—or at least records—from previous summers. Patrons typically do not dwell on summer reading themes as much as librarians do, so there is no reason not to reuse successful program ideas from previous years. (For quick reference, CSLP also keeps a list of its summer reading themes from 1987 to the present on its website at this link: www.cslpreads.org/25-years-of-cslp-themes. iRead's list, dating back to 1982, can be found on its "About" page: www.ireadprogram.org/about.)
- Do without a theme. As mentioned in chapter 2, "Developing a Summer Reading Program," a theme is not a requirement for putting together a successful summer reading program. By simply focusing on reading and offering a selection of unrelated but well-planned activities, you can put on a program that patrons will love without using materials you dislike.

Problems with Prizes

Though they are meant to be enjoyable rewards, summer reading prizes can also cause their share of headaches. This section addresses some of these issues.

It is only the end of June and I have already run out of summer reading prizes. How can I reward the patrons who finish the program between now and the end of the summer?

It can be difficult to predict just how many patrons will participate in summer reading. In summers where your program is more successful than you expected, you might find yourself running low on prizes much earlier than you anticipated. When this happens, it is time to get creative. While you may not be able to provide the prize you originally advertised to every summer reading participant, it should still be possible for you to give each patron something for their efforts. Most patrons will be much more understanding of an alternate prize than a complete lack of a prize.

Assuming that you are unable to purchase additional prizes and that the window for soliciting potential donors has passed, the best replacement for the tangible prizes you can no longer provide are experiential rewards that will present very little cost to the library. These have been described in earlier chapters, especially chapter 3, "Summer Reading Programs for Early Childhood (Ages 0–5)," and chapter 4, "Summer Reading Programs for School-Age Children (Ages 6–12)," but in a situation where resources are scarce, you will want to focus specifically on experiences you can create in the library using supplies you already have on hand and that can be put together relatively quickly.

For the sake of good customer service, do not try to downplay or hide the fact that you have run out of prizes. While patrons are likely to be disappointed when they learn they will not be taking home the book, toy, or other item they anticipated, it is better to prepare them for this disappointment than to blindside them with the news when they arrive to claim their rewards. Replace promotional items in the library and online that advertise the original prize, and use social media and other outlets to inform your community of the new reward. Be prepared for some patrons to react negatively, and perhaps even angrily, but accept their criticism graciously and without becoming defensive. Then when you plan for next year, you can make the appropriate adjustments to prevent the same situation from occurring again.

Patrons are complaining about the prizes my library is offering this year. It is too late to make a change. What should I do?

Though libraries try very hard to do so, it is impossible to please everyone all of the time. Sometimes, for reasons you just do not anticipate, patrons express disappointment and even anger over the items selected as summer reading rewards. In cases where the prize is food (a candy bar, for example, or a coupon for ice cream or donuts), patrons may complain that the chosen item is not healthy or does not match their dietary needs. When the library gives out books, complaints might involve a lack of diversity of genre or reading level among the available options. Even when the prize is tickets to a museum or sporting event, there may be patrons who are not interested in museums or sports who feel excluded.

Whatever the reason, the best thing to do when your summer reading prizes are rejected by your community is to acknowledge your patrons' disappointment, allow them to share with you whatever comments they wish to make, and let them know you will take their concerns into account when planning for the next year's program. Always allow patrons to refuse the reward, and try not to take it personally if their comments are especially negative. Even the most carefully chosen summer reading prize can be a disappointment to someone, but for every patron who dislikes a given reward, there are dozens of other patrons who do appreciate and enjoy it.

I suspect that some of my patrons are cheating in the summer reading contest in order to win a prize without having to work for it. How can I put a stop to this behavior?

It seems that no matter the context, if there is a competition involved, some people will feel compelled to cheat. In a summer reading program, cheating can take a variety of forms: claiming to have read books that the patron did not actually read, reading very short books to inflate reading totals, collecting prizes from multiple library branches, and even lying about a child's age to allow him or her to compete with younger kids, thereby giving that child a competitive edge. Cheating is offensive to librarians' sense of fairness, and it causes many to worry about how their honest patrons are impacted by dishonest participants.

Some of the problems related to cheating can be eliminated simply by the way you structure your summer reading program. For example, if you are concerned that patrons will report dishonestly about the books they have read in order to gain an edge over other patrons, you can design a program that eliminates competition between participants. Instead patrons can compete against objective benchmarks or their own personal goals. While some might still lie to win a prize, in this situation their cheating does not harm anyone else or the integrity of the reading contest overall.

Another way to discourage cheating is to cut back on the type of expensive prizes that might make cheating seem worth it. Some patrons will be willing to cheat in order to win a large prize but would not bother if the prize were merely a token of appreciation. You can also temper patrons' urges to cheat by selecting prize winners by lottery from those who complete the contest. This may discourage potential cheaters looking for an easy win, and it also makes it less likely that any patron you suspect of cheating will be the one chosen to win a prize.

Aside from efforts to prevent cheating in the first place, there is not much a librarian can do about a patron who cheats in the summer reading program. Even if you are nearly certain that a particular participant is cheating, there is no graceful way to approach such a patron without appearing unprofessional or putting yourself in an awkward situation where your word is pitted against the patron's. In general, it is poor form to accuse a patron of cheating or to devise methods for catching him or her in the act. Frustrating as it is, cracking down on the few potential cheaters who might participate in summer reading is simply not a productive use of your time.

I have been contacted by a patron from outside of my library's service area who claims he or she has completed our summer reading program. Do I have to give this patron a prize?

Libraries' web presences and the increasing use of digital software programs for registering summer reading participants and tracking their progress has made it very easy for individuals from anywhere in the country to sign up for your local summer reading program. Some patrons may do this as a prank, but others may sincerely wish to participate and just not realize the limitations of an individual library's summer reading supplies. However the patron has come to be involved in your summer reading program, you have an obligation to represent your library in the most welcoming and positive way possible. When a summer reading participant from outside your community approaches you about collecting a summer reading prize, you should

1. Congratulate them for completing the program.
2. Let them know of your library's policy about out-of-district summer reading participants (e.g., only residents of your service area are eligible to win prizes).
3. Provide a small token to acknowledge completion of the program, such as a printable certificate.
4. Update the language in your summer reading program's promotional materials to prevent a similar situation in future summers.

In some situations, an out-of-area patron might become belligerent and might begin repeatedly contacting you by email or by phone to demand further explanation. If this happens, it is perfectly acceptable to stop responding after you have completed steps 1–3 above. If the individual persists to the point of harassment, it is then appropriate to involve administration or law enforcement as fits the situation.

Problems with Performers

In this section, learn how to troubleshoot difficulties that may arise when hiring paid performers to put on events at your library.

What should I do when I hire a paid performer and no one shows up for the event?

While most librarians have experienced a situation where no one shows up for a scheduled library activity, it can be very frustrating and embarrassing to have this happen when the event involves a paid performer and not just the library's own staff. If at all possible, the best way to handle this type of situation is to take every measure to prevent it from happening in the first place. Chapter 2, "Developing a Summer Reading Program," discusses several ways to maximize attendance at events, including scheduling events during group visits to the library or at times when the library tends to be very busy and choosing performers who suit the specific interests of the audience you hope to reach. While there is never an absolute guarantee of an audience, it helps if you can strategically schedule the event at a time when patrons are likely to participate.

Another way to prevent a situation where an event does not have an audience is to require patrons to register for the event ahead of time and possibly even ask them to print tickets and present them at the door. Patrons sometimes have a tendency to treat drop-in events in a very relaxed manner and they do not commit to attending. If you have them reserve their spaces, however, sometimes they take their attendance more seriously and make an effort to show up. If patrons are preregistered, you also have a way of contacting them in the days leading up to the event to remind them to come. By the same token, if no one registers ahead of time, you can easily cancel the event and save the performer the effort of coming to the library for no reason.

Unfortunately, even the best laid plans can go awry, and all the preventative measures you put in place can still fail. In that situation, although it can be challenging, you may still be able to salvage your event. Even when patrons have not shown up specifically for the event you have planned, there may be individuals in the library at the time of the event who would still be interested in participating. If it looks like attendance will be sparse, make an announcement to patrons letting them know the event is soon to begin and that there are available seats. You can also walk through the library—or even out onto the street if you have a good amount of foot traffic going by—and personally invite potential participants to join the event. As much as possible, you should try to avoid looking desperate or begging people to attend, but there is no harm in asking those who are already visiting the library if they would like to stick around and see your paid performer.

If all else fails, the only other thing you can do is apologize to your performer and see that they are thanked and paid for their time. Performers who have worked with public libraries for any length of time are probably aware that library patrons sometimes do not show up for events even when librarians make every effort to advertise. In most cases, though they may share in your disappointment, they will be understanding and gracious about the situation.

What should I do when a paid performer cancels at the last minute or fails to show up for an event?

As hard as librarians often work to secure audiences for events put on by paid performers, there are situations when, for a variety of reasons, the performers themselves do not show up. Whether this is caused by a last-minute emergency, a miscommunication, or simple forgetfulness, it can be very intimidating for a librarian to have to face an expectant audience and let them know a performance will not be going as scheduled. There are two main ways to handle this situation that will help you manage your audience's disappointment.

The first is to always have a backup program ready to go. In most cases, librarians are not able to exactly replicate the event that a paid performer would have put on, but their programming skills should make it possible to present an activity their patrons will still enjoy. Depending on the intended audience of the performer who did not show up and the particular talents of the librarian coordinating the event, these activities may include storytelling, story times, craft projects, film screenings, musical performances, or book talks. If possible, try to have a backup plan that is thematically similar to the performance you have scheduled, as this will ease the disappointment of your patrons. Still, even if your backup activity is completely different from what was advertised, it is better to offer some activity than to offer nothing.

The second way you can prepare yourself to handle this situation is to write up an announcement for a staff member to read to your audience when a performer does not show up on the day of an event. By writing out an announcement—including an apology to patrons for the disappointment—you never have to worry about becoming flustered and not knowing what to say in the stressful moment when you realize the performer you hired is not going to show up. The prewritten announcement also allows you to think ahead about what you want to say so that the delivery can be as diplomatic and upbeat as possible.

My library has a small budget and we cannot afford to hire any paid performers. How can I provide quality events for my patrons?

While it can often seem as though paid performers make or break a successful summer reading program, this is usually not the case. If your library is not able to afford a professional summer reading performer, there are still ways for you to provide excellent and interesting events for your patrons at low or no cost.

One possibility is to look for organizations in your community that might be able to donate their time and talents in exchange for free publicity and the chance to meet their own outreach goals. Examples might include music schools, martial arts and yoga studios, local artists and authors, and craftsmen. Organizations like these often offer free demonstrations, which can be a great way to add variety to your summer reading program and to help support local businesses.

Another source of potential performers is your local teen population. Many teens have interesting extracurricular hobbies that they would happily teach to younger children or even to fellow teens or adults. Examples include anything from sports skills and magic tricks to craft projects and art techniques. Though it might be nice to pay each teen a small stipend, there will undoubtedly also be some teens who would happily help out just for the experience.

Finally, if all else fails, librarians can rely on each other. If you and several other area librarians are in the same situation regarding funding for summer events, help each other out by planning a program exchange. In this situation, each of you plan an activity to do with a particular patron group, and then you each take turns presenting the event for each other's patrons. Since each librarian is already putting on the event at her own library, there is no extra work involved, and because the libraries are exchanging programs, the cost is limited to the price of materials.

⊚ Youth Services Challenges

This final set of questions and answers focuses on the specific challenges faced by librarians who work with children and teens during the summer reading program. These include problems related to working with schools, camps, and parents.

The local schools will not allow me to visit in order to promote summer reading. How else can I reach the students in my library's service area?

The end of the school year is a busy time for administrators, teachers, and students. Sometimes due to scheduling conflicts or simply being short of time, schools are unable to accommodate visits to or from the public library. When you reach out to schools to offer a visit and they decline, there are still strategies you can use to promote summer reading to students in your community.

One possibility is to reach out to individual teachers to inquire about visiting their classrooms. While the principal or school librarian may not be able to help organize a school-wide visit, you may find that certain teachers, especially in the early elementary grades, are more than happy to have you meet with their students within the context of their own classroom schedules. While this approach does not guarantee that you will reach every student, it does give you a foot in the door with at least some families, which is better than simply not working with the school at all.

If you simply cannot get face time with students, the next best thing to do is to drop off or send summer reading materials to your local schools. These can include any of the promotional materials mentioned in chapter 7, "Promoting Your Summer Reading Program," such as flyers, bookmarks, magnets, and video presentations. You should still contact the school prior to delivering these materials, as they may require approval from an administrator and a representative from the school will most likely have to coordinate their distribution. Still, the school may find it more convenient to distribute promotional materials than to have library staff take up class time with a visit.

Finally, even if working with the local schools is not possible, all is not lost. Instead of visiting schools to promote summer reading, consider other organizations that serve schoolkids during afternoon, evening, and weekend hours. By thinking outside the box and planning visits to after-school programs, scout troops, sports teams, tutoring centers, and the like, you can still reach many of the students who attend your local schools even without involving the school system itself.

A local camp keeps showing up at the library unannounced, expecting a librarian-led activity. How can I stop these surprise visits?

Sometimes camps and similar organizations that make use of the library in the summer are not fully aware of how libraries are run. This can lead the directors of these groups to have unrealistic expectations about how much individualized attention a librarian can give to their members when they visit. To handle the frustration of surprise visits from demanding groups, use some of these tips:

- Introduce yourself to all camps before the problem arises. When camps or other groups enter your library for the first time, do your best to take a free moment to introduce yourself. Having a flyer on hand that explains how you can help serve them is a great way to make your expectations known before any assumptions can be made and to give the group leaders a chance to familiarize themselves with library policy before simply showing up expecting an activity to be available. Introducing yourself also helps promote a friendly relationship between the library and the camp, which sets the tone for the two organizations working together all summer.

- Do not overpolice their activities. Any individual or group who complies with library policy ought to feel free to visit the public library any time it is open. When you approach a camp director, do not make an issue out of the camp visiting the library. Instead, focus on when you are (and are not) available to lead an activity for the group. Share with the group leaders how they can make an appointment for you to meet with their members, and make it clear that your staff just does not have the luxury of accommodating last-minute walk-in groups for anything more than typical library use that does not require a staff member's undivided attention.
- Inform camps of scheduled events. Sometimes camp counselors and those in similar positions do not realize they are permitted to bring their large groups to your regularly scheduled library events. In cases where these organizations are simply looking for ways to keep their groups engaged during camp, their leaders may jump at the chance to bring the campers to your event. Having camps join your scheduled events has the added benefit of helping you avoid situations where particular events do not attract an audience.

Students from an area school have been coming to my library all summer asking for an out-of-print title that is not on our shelves. How should I approach this situation?

When schools provide students with summer reading lists, they often do so on the assumption that students will be able to obtain the listed books from the public library. When this turns out not to be the case, whether due to a title being weeded or to a book list not being updated for several years (or decades), patrons and librarians both can quickly become frustrated. If such a book is not on your library shelves, these approaches may be helpful:

- Search for the book outside of your library. If the book in question is not available from your library branch or system, the next logical step is to find out whether it can be delivered to your library via interlibrary loan or borrowed by the patron from a neighboring library system where your patrons have reciprocal borrowing privileges. If the patron really needs the book, he or she will often be willing to travel a bit further or to pay any applicable interlibrary loan fees.
- Supply the students with a note explaining the situation. Sometimes the school representatives who create summer reading lists do not realize how difficult it can be to find a certain title. One way to help your patrons get this message across to their schools is to provide each student who needs the book with a short form letter explaining that the book is no longer (or perhaps has never been) available from your library. When multiple students show up to school with these letters, the creators of the summer reading lists may decide to change the list for the following year. Notes of this type also help assuage the feelings of guilt that some students and parents might feel when they find themselves unable to fulfill a school requirement by showing that they have done their due diligence.
- Contact a school representative. In some situations, you may have a connection to a teacher or librarian from the school that has assigned the book. In this case,

reaching out to him or her personally might be the best way to explain the difficulties associated with finding the needed title. For this approach to be effective, your contact should be someone directly involved with the creation of summer reading lists or someone who can easily get in contact with such a person. You should also be aware that not all school faculty members are available through their usual communication channels over the summer. Email is probably the most reliable way to reach out, but if there is no response after a reasonable amount of time has passed, you may have to wait until school begins again to sort out the situation.

- Work toward collaborating on summer reading lists. If there has been an ongoing problem with titles from school summer reading lists not being available in your library, it can be helpful to offer to assist in the creation of the lists for the following year. Some schools will be reluctant to accept the help, but others will undoubtedly be grateful, especially if they encourage patrons to borrow the assigned titles from the public library. This approach obviously does not help an individual student in the moment, but it can help to prevent future problems for other students.

I try to encourage kids to read whatever they want during the summer, but some parents place restrictions on their children's reading. How can I encourage them to let their kids read what they would like to read?

There is a fine line between encouraging kids to read what they want during summer reading and pitting children against their parents. While it is admirable for the library to encourage reading in any form and to count all types of reading toward the summer reading program, it is really not a librarian's business to comment on the way a parent chooses to raise his or her children. When a child visits the library with his or her parents, the parents are in charge of that child, and they are free to exercise whatever degree of control they deem necessary over a child's reading material. If the parent has a misconception about the type of reading the library will allow a child to count toward a reading contest, then certainly do not hesitate to explain the rules of the program more clearly. You should not, however, approach a patron with a lot of literature and research about the value of free choice in the development of a child's reading habits unless explicitly asked. To force this information on a parent simply because you disagree with their ideas about what their child should read is unprofessional and could result in the family becoming offended and dropping out of the program altogether.

Parents have been leaving children at summer reading events with no supervision. How can we let these parents know that they need to remain with their children?

Parents sometimes misunderstand library policies about unattended children, and this problem becomes more prevalent in the summer, when kids are not in school. To help parents and other caregivers comply with the library's expectations, try some of these tips:

- Avoid giving your summer reading program a misleading name. Sometimes when a library identifies its summer reading program as a club or a camp, parents get the idea that it is not just a typical library program but a larger function of the library that includes childcare. If this is a common misconception in your community, it is worth considering rebranding your program to alleviate the confusion.
- Share expectations with parents during registration. When parents bring their young children to the library to register for summer reading, it is a good practice to explain to them the details of the program, even those that you perceive to be common sense. During this conversation, make it known what library policy

requires in terms of supervision and inform caregivers outright that library staff are not available to supervise children. Reinforce this information by including it in all printable and digital materials promoting the summer reading program and posting it prominently at all summer reading events.

- Let library policy be your guide. When all else fails, if a parent truly seems to be taking advantage of the library as a source of free childcare or just simply refuses to follow the rules, it is appropriate to take whatever action is prescribed by your library's policy for when a patron violates a rule. Since the consequences of repeatedly leaving a child unattended in the library are sometimes serious (e.g., contacting the police or child services), it is best to notify a supervisor before taking action and to carefully document everything you do so there is a record for posterity.

⊚ Key Points

This chapter has provided a variety of tips for handling difficult situations during your summer reading program.

- Whenever possible, take measures to prevent problems in your summer reading program before they arise.
- Communicating proactively about your summer reading program can prevent misunderstandings with camp counselors, parents, and schools.
- It is best to allow patrons to determine their own level of involvement in the summer reading program. Some will naturally want to be more involved than others.
- Email and text reminders can be a helpful way to keep patrons interested in the summer reading program for its duration.
- In situations where patrons may be disappointed by something that happens in your summer reading program, be open, honest, and diplomatic in your communication.

Congratulations! Having read to the end of this book, you are now fully equipped to take on the challenge of planning and implementing successful summer reading programs for patrons of all ages. May your library enjoy many wonderful summers!

Index

About the Author

Katie Fitzgerald holds a bachelor's degree in English from Vassar College and a master's degree in information science from the University at Albany, State University of New York. She has worked in the Josephine-Louise Public Library in Walden, New York, as well as the Tenley-Friendship branch of the DC Public Library, and she is the author of *Story Time Success: A Practical Guide for Librarians*. She also writes about story time and library service on her blog, *Story Time Secrets* (http://storytimesecrets.blogspot.com/).